Contents

Ward Lock's Encyclopedia of MUSIC

Alan Blackwood

VICTOR CARPATHIVS

Ward Lock's
Encyclopedia of
MUSIC
Alan Blackwood

Ward Lock Limited·London

© Text Alan Blackwood 1979

© Colour illustrations Fabbri Editori S.p.A. 1979

First published in Great Britain in 1979
by Ward Lock Limited, 116 Baker Street,
London, W1M 2BB, a Pentos Company.

Typeset in Monophoto Bembo by
Asco Trade Typesetting Ltd, Hong Kong

Printed and bound in Italy by
Fabbri Editori S.p.A.

British Library Cataloguing in Publication Data

Blackwood, Alan, *b.1932*
    Ward Lock's encyclopaedia of music.
    1. Music—Dictionaries, Juvenile
    I. Title
    II. Encyclopaedia of music
    780'.3   ML100

ISBN 0-7063-5795-7

Introduction

A large orchestra tuning up before a concert is an exciting sound. It creates a wonderful mood of expectancy, a sense of great things about to happen. Then the conductor takes his place on the rostrum, raises his baton, and with one accord the orchestra leads us into that special world of sound called music.

Many people believe that a sense of music is our most basic and intuitive means of expression. From time immemorial men have summoned up courage to fight their enemies or hunt wild beasts with the cry of their voices, the clap of their hands and the stamp of their feet; they have sung and chanted to keep up their strength and powers of endurance during long hours of back-breaking work; they have shouted and danced in triumph, wailed in moments of grief or pain and sung to express their joy or their sorrow in love. From the war cry to the soft croon of a mother to her baby, music has always seemed our instinctive response to our deepest and strongest feelings.

In times past this belief in the special powers of music gave rise to many famous stories or legends. According to the Bible, music had the power to bring down the walls of Jericho. In Greek mythology Orpheus could pacify the fiercest creatures through the enchantment of his music. Other ancient legends from India and China speak of the power of music to change the seasons, even to create fire and water. The people of pre-Christian Mexico believed there was a bridge high over the sky by which music came down from heaven.

The power of music exalts this American Indian fire dancer.

7

Less fanciful was the belief of Plato, Aristotle and other great thinkers of ancient Greece in the power of music for both good and ill. They praised some music as noble and uplifting and condemned other types of music as bad for the soul. Most interesting of all is the age-old belief that the Sun, Moon, Earth and other planets are ordered according to strict mathematical proportions; and that the mathematics of music relates to this cosmic order in a special way. The Chinese philosopher Confucius was probably referring to this idea when he spoke of music conveying 'the accord of Heaven and Earth'. The Greek philosopher and mystic Pythagoras shared with others of his time the even more fascinating idea that this special relationship between the mathematical order of the universe and of music took the form of a divine 'music of the spheres'. According to this idea each of the planets generates a particular sound or note. These notes cannot be heard by us in the ordinary sense, but they are none the less sounding everywhere and all the time, harmonizing the order and motion of the planets.

The 'music of the spheres' remains a beautiful but unproven theory. The mathematics of sound, however, is real enough, and of great value to our better understanding of the way in which music works. The source of musical sounds, and of all other sounds, is some kind of vibration. This is transmitted to the surrounding medium, such as water or air, and travels through it in a series of what are usually called waves, though 'pulses' is a better word to describe what happens. These waves or pulses of sound continue to travel through the air, water or other medium until their energy is exhausted and they fade away. But if our ears intercept them first, then our ear drums start to vibrate in

Temple dancer from ancient Egypt. In the great civilizations of the past music had a deep religious and mystical meaning.

sympathy and our brains interpret this activity as sound.

The importance of this to music is that the rapidity of the sound waves is directly related to the PITCH (the 'highness' or 'lowness') of a note. The faster or more rapid the vibrations, the higher the pitch of the note; and since it is possible to measure this rapidity and express it in terms of a number of vibrations per second, its so-called FREQUENCY, so the pitch of every musical note can be expressed as a number. A very significant number in this context is 440. By international agreement this has been fixed as the frequency for the note A above Middle C, and all instruments should be tuned to this note in order to play at what is called 'concert pitch'.

Pitch, of course, is the factor that determines our present system of NOTATION or written music. This is now based on five parallel lines, called staff lines or STAVES, drawn horizontally across a page, and notes are written on or between these staves to represent their pitch. The higher they are placed, the higher is their pitch. Exactly what the pitch of the notes should be is indicated by the CLEF sign. There are two clefs now in common use, treble and bass, though a few instruments make use of one of the third and fourth called the alto and the tenor clefs, which come between treble and bass as far as range of pitch is concerned (a fifth clef, the soprano, occurs in some old choral music). A note written on the first stave in the treble clef, for example, is much higher in pitch than one written on the first stave of the bass clef.

Simple mathematics can also help us to understand the matter of musical TIMBRE—of what gives a note its particular quality and enables us to distinguish easily between the sound of, say, a violin and a trumpet, or between the sounds of our own voices. Such different qualities are in fact created by the number and type of overtones. A flute, for instance, makes a very pure sound because it has few overtones, while the human voice has a warm quality which is due to

A battered but fascinating fragment of Egyptian papyrus believed to contain the words and melody of a love song.

its many overtones. To understand how these overtones occur, we may take the case of the violin. Every time the effective playing length of one of the strings starts to vibrate, it does so not only along its entire length, but in fractions of that length—a half, thirds, quarters and o on. We are usually only aware of the pitch of the note, called the 'fundamental', produced by the violin string as it vibrates along its entire playing length; but our ears are also picking up the differently pitched sounds produced by the fractional vibrations of the string, and it is the way these overtones, some louder than others, blend that creates for us the timbre of the note. Exactly the same principle applies to wind instruments, where it is a column of air in a tube that vibrates along its entire playing length and along fractions of that length.

There is nothing mysterious about these overtones, or natural HARMONICS as they are also called. In wind instruments, especially brass ones, the natural harmonics are quite easy to discover, as anyone who plays a bugle will know. By blowing harder, or slightly altering the pressure of his lips against the mouthpiece, the bugler can obtain the basic notes of the instrument's harmonic series—all the old military bugle calls are selected from these same few notes. What is miraculous, however, is the way our ears and brain can receive and interpret, every second, millions of sounds of different pitch and strength, which is what we do with no conscious effort every time we listen to an orchestra.

We may think of the natural harmonics of an instrument like the bugle as a kind of scale—the series of notes available to the player. The word SCALE comes from the Italian *scala* meaning 'step', and is a good word for describing any pre-arranged series of notes spaced out in ascending or descending order of pitch. Within our own system of notation the notes of a scale, placed on or between the staves, do indeed look very like a flight of steps.

Another way of considering scales is as the building blocks of music. They are the range of notes actually available to the musician to build up as melodies and harmonies. There are many

Another temple dancer, this time from Bangkok. Every movement of her body conveys some special meaning.

different scales, or systems of scales. The pentatonic ('five-toned') scale is one. This happens to correspond, in terms of intervals of pitch, with the black notes on a piano keyboard, and is the basis of much folk music, including music for the Scottish bagpipes. However, the group of scales most familiar to us in the so-called Western world are those which we call the diatonic scales.

The easiest of these diatonic scales to play on the piano is the one that starts on any note C (usually middle C) and proceeds upwards by each white note in turn until the next C is reached. The INTERVAL between the two C notes is called an OCTAVE, because there are eight notes in the scale. In acoustical terms, the frequency of the upper C should, if the piano is properly tuned, be exactly twice that of the lower C. The interval of the octave also happens to be the first interval in any harmonic series.

The first, or key note of a scale is called the TONIC. Thus the tonic note of our scale of C is C and the tonic of the scale of D is D. The succeeding notes progress upwards by precise intervals called whole tones or semitones (which are half tones). They can be related to the tonic by calling them the third note of the scale, the fourth, the fifth and so on. Alternatively, they can be related to the tonic by names which describe their special place in the scale. For example, the fifth note up from the tonic is the dominant, the fourth note is the sub-dominant, the third note is the mediant.

The beauty of the diatonic arrangement of a scale lies in the fact that it can be applied equally well to any of the twelve available starting or tonic notes. All that needs to be done is to raise (sharpen) or lower (flatten) by a semitone one or more of the notes used in our scale of C, so that the intervals of each note of the new scale remain constant in relation to the tonic and to each other. A piece of music based on any of these scales is said to be in the KEY of that scale, and at the beginning of the written music the 'key signature' reminds us which notes much be sharpened or flattened in order to keep the music true to the notes of that scale.

The scale of C described above, and any of the other twelve scales similarly organised, are more precisely called 'major' scales. There are twelve corresponding 'minor' scales which are basically obtained by flattening (lowering by a semitone) the third note of any major scale. This is only a small tonal alteration, but it is enough to make the character of major and minor scales and keys quite different. Some people say that major scales, and pieces of music based on them, are optimistic and happy in mood, while minor scales and minor-key music are sad or even tragic. There is some truth in this, though the distinction is not really as simple and clear-cut as that.

What is important is the way that most music based on the diatonic scales and keys, major and minor, depends upon the tonic note of the key. If a piece of music is in the key of C major, then it often both starts and finishes on the note or chord of C. The tonic is, in fact, rather like an anchor. In a nursery rhyme tune like 'Baa Baa Black Sheep', or some of the old familiar hymn tunes, the MELODY and harmonies never move far from the tonic. In a Beethoven symphony, by contrast, the music might leave the tonic far behind and MODULATE, or 'move', into other keys as it sets out on some great harmonic adventure; but even with Beethoven the force of the tonic is always there, and by the end of the symphony the music will have returned obediently to its home key of the tonic.

So strong, indeed, is this harmonic feature of diatonic music that we quite instinctively listen all the time for the return to the tonic, whether as the last note of a tune or a chord. In church, for example, many people would be most upset if a hymn tune did not end on a satisfying sequence of chords of the 'amen' type though they probably could not explain why. However, as we shall read shortly, other systems of scales and harmonies, equally valid, existed for hundreds of years before our diatonic major and minor scales and keys were introduced. In this century many composers have found new and exciting ways of writing music that owe little or nothing to our deep-seated ideas about the tonic.

Melody, which is a progression of notes, and

HARMONY, which lies behind the shaping of melody and may give it support by the sounding of other notes and chords, are two of the basic ingredients of music. The third is RHYTHM. Rhythm is the beat or underlying pulse of music, giving it coherence and momentum. Some people claim it to be the most potent and powerful of all our musical responses, instilled into us even before we are born by the beat of our mother's heart.

In our Western society we have largely tamed and rationalized this rhythmic sense. We divide rhythms into regular sections called BARS, and classify them as having two or three beats, or combinations of these, to the bar. Within these bars, or measures, we then distribute notes of carefully calculated duration. As a part of this system, the CROTCHET is taken as the standard note of duration, and other notes of duration are either shorter (the QUAVER and SEMIQUAVER) or longer (the MINIM and SEMIBREVE) by fractions or multiples of two. Military marches and some types of dance are very strict about the way they keep to three or four beats to the bar, neatly and precisely spacing out the rhythm with crotchets or the equivalent number of minims or quavers. Most of us, though, are happy and willing to take a much freer attitude to rhythm. The great popularity of jazz and Latin American music, which had its origins in the tribal societies of West Africa, and of the dance and rock music following from it, testifies to this.

In many societies other than our own, in fact, rhythm is not marked by any kind of regular bar or measure; but the lack of a regular beat, as we may think of it, does not reflect any lack of rhythmic sense. Such societies simply use rhythm in a different way, often to very potent effect. In parts of the Middle East and North Africa, for example, religious dancers called dervishes can work themselves into a complete state of trance through the power of rhythm. We may find it difficult to follow the beat of such rhythms, but they can make the dervishes dance and whirl until they fall almost lifeless to the ground.

Many composers this century have become interested in the often very complex rhythms of the Middle East and Far East as a way of giving their own music a new sense of rhythmic freedom. Igor Stravinsky provided an early lead in this field with the score to his ballet *The Rite of Spring*, depicting pagan rites and dances in ancient Russia. In this composition Stravinsky does not dispense with bars, but in certain passages of the music he achieves an extraordinary sense of rhythmic complexity and power by constantly changing the beat from one bar to the next. Today this famous piece of twentieth-century music is as much a favourite with many concert-goers as the works of Bach, Mozart, Beethoven, Schubert or Brahms, rousing audiences to a pitch of excitement, as though the spirit of our ancient pagan past were still strong within us.

Carved wooden tom tom player from Zaire in Africa. Something of his rhythms lives on in jazz and modern rock music.

History

Much of the early music of the Christian era—generally taken to mark the beginning of our so-called Western musical tradition—was founded on PLAINSONG, or plainchant, which had neither rhythm in the usual sense nor harmony. It grew out of the kind of chanting used by the Jews in their religious ceremonies—just as Christianity grew from Judaism—but was based on a group of scales called MODES, which had their origins in the music of ancient Greece. Each of these modes consisted of eight notes, like our scales today, but they were organized differently. Whereas modern major and minor scales all follow the same pattern of intervals between the notes, each mode had its own special sequence of intervals. To know what they sounded like you can play the white notes on the piano, first from one C note to the next C note an octave higher, then from one D note to the octave D above, and so on. In this way it is easy to hear how the sequence of intervals between the notes changes slightly but significantly each time, giving each mode its own unique sound and character.

In the history of early Western music there were originally four modes. These were introduced towards the end of the fourth century AD by St Ambrose, Bishop of Milan, who wished to establish a standard form of music for use among the various branches of the still young and rapidly expanding Christian church. Two hundred years later Pope Gregory I approved the use of four more modes, and finally, during the sixteenth century, a Swiss monk named Henry of Glarus added a further four.

Plainsong itself was a type of chant that set to music various parts of the church liturgy (the words of the church services), psalms and other religious texts. It consisted of a single line of melody which progressed in gentle, undramatic steps up and down the notes of one or other of the modes. Plainsong was sung in unison (which means that everybody sang the same note), and in its pure form was unadorned by any kind of accompaniment. Because it followed the stress and flow of whatever text it was set to, it had no steady beat. The Ambrosian and the more famous Gregorian chant were the two main forms of plainsong and the principal type of European music for a large part of the Middle Ages, starting from the time of the break-up of the Roman Empire when the churches and monasteries of Christendom were the new centres of European art and learning. Such music was not composed in our modern sense of the word, but arranged and performed by generations of anonymous monks and churchmen, as one of their daily duties. Something of its character remains in the sung prayers and responses still to be heard in church services today.

In the original plainsong the religious text was supposed to be of far greater importance than the music, which was restricted by the need to follow the words syllable by syllable. However, in the course of time changes came about in the singing of plainsong, prompted by the choristers' desire to give the music more life of its own. Sometimes the singers would add extra notes to a particular word or syllable, or else a few extra

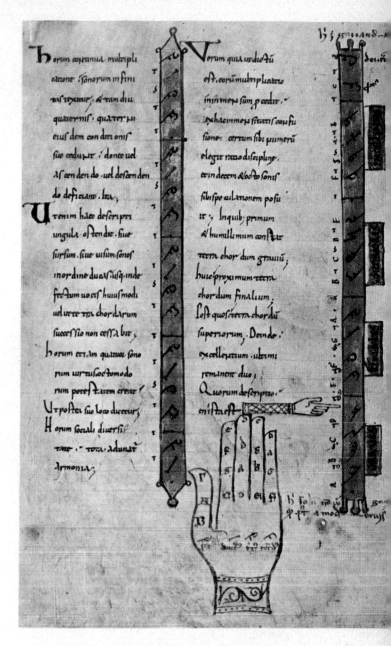

Above: Page from a famous ninth-century manuscript presenting new ideas about singing and harmony. The signs written against the text are neumes, an early system of notation. The hand bearing the alphabetical names of notes was a common feature of medieval treatises on music. A Flemish monk named Hucbald (about 840–930) was once thought to be the author of this work. Scholars now doubt this, though Hucbald was an important figure in early medieval music.
Left: Image of Pope Gregory the Great, one of the founding figures of European music. Carved in ivory, and dating from the ninth century, this is a fine example of Carolingian art— that relating to the time of Charlemagne (744–814).

Two illustrations from illuminated manuscripts. *Left:* two psaltery players. This was an ancient stringed instrument, plucked like a harp but with a sounding board. *Above:* King David playing bells. He was widely featured in medieval decoration, as one of the greatest musicians in the Bible.

words would be included at those places in the liturgy where it was felt that this would help the flow of the melody. Practices of this sort were called TROPES and with the coming of notation collections of them were recorded in books or manuscripts known as tropers.

Tropes were one way of bringing more freedom to plainsong melody. Of far greater significance was the start of a type of harmonized singing called ORGANUM. At its simplest, organum was the singing of a second line of melody at a constant pitch interval to the original melody, both melodic lines proceeding rather like parallel railway tracks. This very basic organum singing was, in fact, called 'strict' or 'parallel' organum. Free organum, developing from it, allowed the two melodic lines greater independence, so that they became much more like two distinct strands of melody. Then came

the introduction of a third or forth melodic line, and a much more imaginative intermingling of these lines or parts. All this, in turn, called for a stronger sense of musical rhythm, a steady beat being required to guide and control the progress of the parts. These changes took place over a period of several hundred years, from about the ninth to the twelfth centuries, and led to one of the greatest and longest surviving styles of music, POLYPHONY.

'Polyphony' is a Greek word meaning 'many sounds', and it entails the weaving together of two or more melodic lines, or parts. With its development European music became a true art form, and musicians emerged who were no longer simply arrangers but were composers in their own right. The most famous centre of early polyphonic composition was the Notre Dame School in Paris, so called because it was associated

Two more musicians from illuminated manuscripts. *Above:* Bagpipers. *Right:* Hurdy-gurdy players. They are turning the handle with one hand and stopping the strings with the other. Both the hurdy-gurdy and the bagpipes have an ancient and colourful history, especially in the field of folk music.

with the planning and building of the great Gothic cathedral. Two of the earliest composers to be remembered by name were associated with the Notre Dame School. They were Léonin (or Leoninus, to give the Latin form of his name) and his successor Pérotin (or Perotinus).

One notable feature of this early music is the way it was based on the pitch intervals of the octave, the fourth or the fifth notes of one or other of the modes. These, of course, are some of the principal overtones or harmonics of musical sound, and the musicians of the Middle Ages felt instinctively drawn towards them. Like the great stone columns and carvings of the Romanesque and Gothic cathedrals in which it was first heard, their music can convey to us, after nearly a thousand years, the same feeling of an almost timeless strength and wonder which permeates the atmosphere of these splendid churches.

Through the Middle Ages the Church remained the most powerful institution in Europe, and people challenged its authority at their peril. Yet notwithstanding the grim teachings of the medieval Church and despite frequent war, famine and outbreaks of the plague, people knew how to enjoy themselves, and as the Middle Ages progressed so there grew up also a strong tradition of non-religious or secular music.

Dancing, like singing, had been enjoyed throughout Europe from the earliest times. In the medieval period it was so popular that although the church authorities frowned upon it they could not prevent it and even allowed certain dances to be performed on occasions within the church buildings. Elsewhere dances performed by groups of people, from the humble round dances on the village green to the formal court dances of kings and nobles, required musi-

17

Two aspects of medieval chivalry, as expressed in many of the songs of the troubadours and minstrel-knights. *Above:* Knights in combat. *Left:* Courtly love.

cal accompaniment. Voices or instruments such as rebecs, bagpipes, horns, reed pipes, drums and tambourines provided this, and music with regular beat and phrasing, in contrast to religious music with its continuous flow of sound, was developed to suit the requirements of the dance.

Much of the music for the dances of peasants and of nobles was provided by travelling musicians. Professional entertainers, those who could juggle, stand on their hands, turn cartwheels and somersaults and do numerous other things as well as dance, sing and play a variety of musical instruments, had been around in Europe since the days of the Roman Empire, when their Latin name was *joculator*. They were called *jongleurs* in France, gleemen in England, *Gaukler* in Germany, where they were especially renowned for their distinctive costumes, often of red and yellow.

More specialized in music were the minstrels who composed much of their own poetry and song. In Britain and Ireland there had been minstrels going right back to the time of the Druids, that is before the Roman occupation. It was the coming of the Romans that made many of the English Druidic minstrels retreat westwards into Wales. There they held contests of poetry and song, forerunners of the *Eisteddfodau* that are still a lively part of Welsh life and culture. In Germany too there was a strong tradition among minstrels, or *Minnesinger* ('singers of love') as they were called, for holding song and poetry contests. One of the legendary meeting places for these contests, an ancient hilltop castle in Thuringia called the Wartburg, inspired Wagner to compose his opera *Tannhäuser*. For all these minstrels the harp was an important instrument. These were not the large, heavy concert harps of today, but small, portable versions such as the Celtic Welsh telyn and Irish clàrsach, and their soft, rather plaintive tones seem to us beautifully suited to accompany the songs of love and longing so favoured by the minstrels.

Most famous of all these medieval poet-musicians were the troubadours. Their name comes from the old Provençal word *trobar* meaning 'to find' in the sense of finding or inventing poems and tunes. They flourished during the period of the Crusades, and many troubadours, such as Richard I of England called Richard Coeur de Lion, were knights who had been in Palestine to do battle with the armies of Islam over the possession of the Holy Lands of the Bible. Upon their return they composed the words and music to many *chansons de geste* ('songs of heroic deeds'), describing their adventures. The *Chanson de Roland*, well known in literature as well as in music, was one of these. Other songs were on the subject of chivalrous love—of the knight bound by the strictest code of chivalry to honour and defend the virtue of his lady. The troubadours travelled about the warm, vibrant landscapes of Provence and the Languedoc in southern France, their period drawing to a close

Playing and dancing to the tambourine. An instrument of Arabic origin, the tambourine has hardly changed in over six hundred years.

19

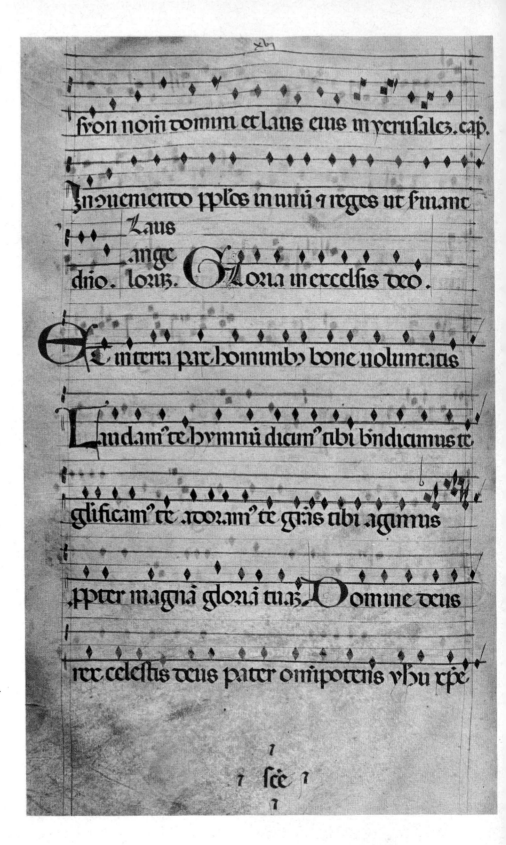

Early staff notation in a medieval illuminated manuscript. The method of using staff lines, or staves, to represent sounds of a particular pitch and placing notes on or between them dates back to the eleventh century and the work of men like Guido d'Arezzo (see also page 141).

during the bitter war against a heretical religious sect called the Albigenses during the thirteenth century. In the rest of France, meanwhile, there were other poet-musicians who went by the equivalent French name of *trouvères*.

The troubadours who returned from the Crusades brought back with them Arabic instruments like the stringed rebec and the lute, and the melodies of their songs often used intervals of pitch that gave them a distinctly Arabic or Oriental sound. Another Arabic influence on European music during the Middle Ages came from Spain, most of which was occupied for hundreds of years by the Moors of North Africa.

The influence of Arabic instruments and melodies was strongest on the songs and dances of the period, but these in turn began to affect the

Fourteenth-century musician playing a portative organ. These instruments could be carried in processions.

church music. The church authorities did not generally approve of the influence of the troubadours on sacred music, but the cross-fertilization of ideas between secular and religious music from about the thirteenth century onwards was of great interest and benefit to Western music as a whole. For example, the tune of one old Provençal song called *L'Homme Armé* ('The Armed Man'), whose original words are lost to us, was used over and over again by fourteenth- and fifteenth-century composers of religious music. There were also many cases of secular and religious music existing side by side in a single composition, each style influencing the other. A celebrated example of this is the Reading Rota, composed at Reading Abbey some time during the thirteenth century. In any event, it is an astonishingly advanced piece of music for its time with a fine sturdy rhythm, and it is written out very cleverly in the polyphonic form of a rota or ROUND, in which the same tune, sung by several different voices, follows itself round and round. Significantly, the piece had two different texts, a religious one in Latin (which was then the accepted language of the Western church) and the now much more familiar one in Old English 'Sumer is icumen in' ('Summer Is A-coming In').

Most musicians of the period were very excited about what was happening. They welcomed the exchange of ideas between religious and secular music and the way that these brought more varied rhythms and flowing melodies to their art, thus increasing its richness. As a sign of this enthusiasm they spoke of their music as *ars nova* (Latin for 'new art'), in contrast to the *ars antiqua* or 'old art' of former times. Philippe de Vitry, one of the most eminent musicians of the fourteenth century, wrote a whole treatise on the subject of this new form of the art. Guillaume de Machaut, another exponent of the *ars nova* style, may also have been the first to compose a complete musical setting of the service of the Mass.

Equally notable was the way that music during the fourteenth and fifteenth centuries often went hand in hand with other important occupations and so gained in status. Philippe de Vitry was a bishop of the church and a diplomat at the French court as well as a musician. Some of the composers who came after him achieved even greater social standing. The Englishman John Dunstable, who spent most of his life in France, was not only a composer of great prestige and influence but also a noted mathematician and astrologer, at a time when astrology was still taken very seriously. Jean de Ockeghem served the French court and was praised by a devoted admirer as 'the sun shining above all others'. One of his pupils, Josquin des Prés, who was soon acknowledged to be one of the most inspired composers of polyphonic church music, became a high-ranking priest. These men lived around the time of the Hundred Years War, the long struggle between the various royal households of France and England, which included the campaigns of Henry V of England and Joan of Arc and brought much devastation and misery in their train. But musicians, like other eminent artists and scholars of the time, were not much affected by these events. They travelled widely and were welcomed almost everywhere.

One great centre of the arts and especially of music was at the court of Dijon, capital of the rich and independent province of Burgundy in eastern France. Philip the Good, Duke of Burgundy, was deeply involved in politics and war, opposing Joan of Arc and the Dauphin (the French heir to the throne) and siding with the English. At the same time he was a generous patron of the arts and his chapel choir was probably the best in Europe. Many of the finest musicians of the age found employment there or in other parts of the province, and are now known collectively as the Burgundians. As depicted in old prints and manuscripts they may seem to us slightly quaint and remote, but in the Europe of their day they were powerful figures and men to be reckoned with.

A time of great trouble and upheaval in church affairs began with the activities of Martin Luther. He was a German priest and monk who in 1517 first publicly attacked what he saw as serious abuses in church life. He went on, with others, to reject the authority of the Pope in Rome and in the following years the Lutheran and other Reformed or Protestant churches were formed. This was the Reformation, and it heralded a long and terrible period of conflict between those people and nations who remained faithful to the Church of Rome—the Roman Catholic

Martin Luther, painted by his fellow countryman Lucas Cranach. The founder of the Reformation was a great scholar and loved music.

Three Singers, a painting by the Italian Renaissance artist Lorenzo Costa. They are singing to the accompaniment of a lute.

Church—and those who went over to the new Protestant churches. In England the conflict was triggered off by a personal quarrel between Henry VIII and the Pope, leading to the establishment of the Church of England.

Despite all this unrest the sixteenth century was a great age for polyphonic church music. Many composers of the period continued to be attracted by the idea of a mystic or divine order in mathematics and sought to worship God through rich and beautiful music which was based most carefully on the complicated mathematics of pitch and of rhythm. There was also, however, a movement towards greater simplicity in church music. This was a part of the so-called Counter-Reformation, which was the Roman Catholic Church's response to the Reformation itself. In 1545 the Pope convened the Council of Trent, held at the town of Trento in northern Italy, to examine various aspects of church life and practice and recommend reforms where these were thought necessary. Church music was on the agenda, and it was harshly criticized, mainly on the grounds that it was often over elaborate and paid too little attention to the meaning or even the audibility of the liturgy. Such music was condemned by the Council as giving only 'empty pleasure to the ear'. Indeed, the whole future of music for church use was called into question.

One composer who helped to save the situation for music was Giovanni Pierluigi da Palestrina. There is a story that it was only his divinely inspired *Missa Papae Marcelli* ('Mass for Pope Marcellus') that saved music in church from actually being banned by the Council. Historians now discount this story, but it is almost certainly the case that the clear, pure sound of Palestrina's choral music and the respect he paid to the words he was setting did much to restore music to favour with the church authorities. Over three hundred years later Wagner, a very different kind of composer, was still moved to write of Palestrina's music as 'timeless and spaceless, a spiritual revelation throughout'.

Luther, on his side, welcomed music in religion. 'It is a gift of God,' he declared. 'Music drives away the Devil and makes people happy.' As a scholar he especially loved the polyphonic music of Josquin des Prés, but decided that for normal church services a new kind of music was needed which the congregation could share to the fullest extent. So he wrote the words, and possibly the music as well, to several new hymns, or CHORALES. The words were not in scholarly Latin but in the every-day language of the people, and the tunes were strong, memorable and easily learnt, so that everybody could join in the singing. *Ein' feste Burg*, usually translated into English as 'A Safe Stronghold' is the most famous of these Lutheran chorales. Known also as 'The Battle Hymn of the Reformation', it is still regularly sung in the various branches of the Lutheran Church.

The Reformation took place against the background of a more general change in European affairs, known as the Renaissance. This French word describes the 'rebirth' or 'reawakening' of interest among scholars and artists in the art,

architecture and literature of the Greeks and Romans—achievements that had been largely neglected or forgotten about during the long period of the Middle Ages. In fact, the Renaissance as we think of it today was a period of about two hundred years, roughly from 1400 to 1600, during which the whole pattern of European civilization underwent big changes. Trade and commerce brought new wealth, while

ni persi   Lò tro me fichato ella

nti diuersi

 èro infelice

Part of the beautifully decorated score of
a sixteenth-century Italian madrigal.
Compare this staff notation with the
earlier example shown on page 20.

philosophy, science and great voyages of dis-
covery changed people's whole outlook on life. It
was the age of Galileo Galilei, Christopher
Columbus, Leonardo da Vinci and William
Shakespeare.

   This new Renaissance outlook had a significant
effect on literature and the arts. Shakespeare's
plays are to do with human feelings and be-
haviour, Leonardo studied anatomy, designed

flying machines and painted portraits of real
people—subjects and themes which reflected a
certain loosening of the hold which the Church
had over society and a quickening interest in life as
it is lived in this world rather than as it might be
lived in the hereafter. In music the situation was
the same. Great religious music continued to be
written throughout the Renaissance period, but
there was a wonderful blossoming of secular

music also. One of the most important types of secular composition, for a small group of voices, was the madrigal. This originated in Italy, home of so much Renaissance thought and practice, but its popularity soon spread abroad. Its early French counterpart was the CHANSON, though the influence of the Italian madrigal lead to the development of a more expressive style and more complicated form. In England Nicholas Yonge, a chorister of St Paul's Cathedral, London, issued a collection of Italian madrigals in 1588—the year of the Spanish Armada—under the title *Musica Transalpina* ('Music from across the Alps'). His enterprise bore marvellous fruit, for there followed a succession of the most inspired madrigals, including the work of such gifted composers as William Byrd, Thomas Morley, Thomas Weelkes, John Wilbye and Orlando Gibbons. One famous edition of their work was issued under the title of *The Triumphs of Oriana*, the name 'Oriana' fancifully referring to Queen Elizabeth I. These madrigals, like those from Italy, express human feelings far more directly than any previous European music; the melody and harmony reflect the meaning of the words and allow the music to 'laugh' and 'weep', and to allude to the world of nature, in ways that earlier composers would hardly have understood. Their composers were contemporaries of Shakespeare, making this a golden age for English music as well as literature.

Another type of secular vocal piece closely associated with the English Elizabethan period was the song or AYRE, arranged either as a part-song or to be performed by a solo singer with instrumental accompaniment. Skilful arrangement was often valued as highly as original composition in Renaissance times, and John Dowland was an outstanding composer and arranger of these ayres. Dowland, who served the royal court of Denmark for some years and was one of the most famous musicians of his day, was also a fine lutenist. The lute, a beautiful looking stringed instrument, plucked like a guitar, was one of many that also mark the Renaissance as the first great period of European instrumental music. Most types of instrument available in the sixteenth century had existed, in one form or another, in the Middle Ages, but their use had been limited mainly to the music of the troubadours, jongleurs and other minstrels. Sometimes an organ or handbells had been used in church to accompany organum and early polyphony, but instruments generally were frowned upon by churchmen (because of associations with ancient pagan civilizations), and their acceptance in church was slow.

The great variety of instruments to be found in most Renaissance royal courts and in the homes of the wealthy included, apart from the lute, wind instruments such as recorders and racketts (ancestors of the bassoon), and bowed stringed instruments, the viols. These were all usually made in sets of four or more, each instrument being designed to encompass a different range of notes, and in performance they were known as a CONSORT. Sometimes individual instruments from different consorts were played together in a 'broken consort', producing a more varied sound. Their existence in such numbers was due both to the new-found skills of Renaissance craftsmen, and to the fact that increasing prosperity through trade and banking gave people more money to spend and more leisure time. Such people liked to play instruments for their own sake, or as an accompaniment to dancing. Two of the most popular court dances of the time were the slow and stately PAVAN and the lively GALLIARD, the same music sometimes being arranged for both. The galliard, especially, lent itself to rapid and skilful footwork, and such pieces were often dedicated to a particular dancer.

In addition to the many wind and stringed instruments that were such proud possessions in Renaissance households, there were early keyboard instruments—virginals and harpsichords. Henry VIII as a young man loved music, and

A fine sixteenth-century organ from Italy. Note the pedal keyboard and stops, or registers, allowing the player to select different combinations of pipes.

Trumpeters in Renaissance Venice. Their music was an important part of the pomp and ceremony of the city in its golden age.

there are royal inventories indicating that he had a virginal or other keyboard instrument installed in practically every room of his various palaces. A famous collection of keyboard pieces, probably compiled during the reign of his daughter Elizabeth I, is now known as the *Fitzwilliam Virginal Book*. Equally famous is the first printed edition of keyboard music published in England in 1611, entitled *Parthenia* ('Maidenhood'), and including pieces by Byrd and Gibbons. Printing, another achievement of the Renaissance period, helped enormously the spread of music as it had done the written word.

The revival of interest in the arts of classical Greece and Rome led to the creation of the first OPERAS. The general idea of opera, as a combination of music and drama, and sometimes of dancing also, was not new to European culture. In the Middle Ages a big feature of town and city life had been the religious or semi-religious Miracle Plays (also called 'Morality' or 'Mystery' plays). These were originally performed inside churches, consisting of a fairly short musical dramatization of some biblical event. As they became longer and more elaborate affairs, so they moved outside the church building, often being presented on the church or cathedral steps during religious festivals. Jongleurs and other performers sometimes joined forces with church musicians; there were constructions which amounted to stage sets representing scenes like the mouth of hell, and altogether they must have been good entertainment. There were also rather more aristocratic entertainments involving poetry, music and dancing, called MASQUES. These usually took a story from classical mythology as their theme.

It was, however, the activities of a group of Italian poets and musicians, known as the *Camerata* ('Fellowship'), who lived in Florence around the year 1600 that are generally taken to mark the beginnings of opera as we think of it today. They believed that the words of classical drama had all been sung, so adopted a way of declaiming them in a singing style called 'monody', (meaning 'single melody') which they hoped was close to the ancient Greek drama they admired. To this monody they added an instrumental accompaniment, consisting mainly of chords, to give harmonic support. Such a musical style was the complete opposite of polyphony with its interweaving of several melodic parts. The word 'opera', which is simply the Latin for 'works', was not used at first. *Dramma musicale* ('musical drama') and *Dramma per musica* ('drama through music') were two of the various names given to it. Nevertheless, musical scholars today consider the earliest surviving example of true opera to be *Euridice*, which was based on the story from Greek mythology about Orpheus and Eurydice. Its composer was Jacopo Peri, a priest in the household of the Medicis, the celebrated Florentine family who had used their wealth and power to rival the Church as patrons of some of the greatest Renaissance artists and scholars.

Claudio Monteverdi, pioneer of opera and of the orchestra.

The magnificence of Versailles, the great Baroque palace where both opera and ballet flourished.

Claudio Monteverdi composed his opera *Orfeo*, based on the same legend, while employed at the court of the Duke of Mantua. He later moved to Venice, most illustrious of all Italian Renaissance city-states due to its position on the main trade route between Europe and the East, to become director of music at St Mark's Cathedral. This famous church had two organs and several galleries, and had inspired a style of music noted for the way in which separate groups of singers or instrumentalists 'answered' each other from various parts of the building to create dramatic contrasts of sound. Music of this kind is called ANTIPHONAL, from the Greek word meaning 'sounding across'. Monteverdi's predecessor, Giovanni Gabrieli, chief organist at St Mark's, was a famed composer of such music, notably for groups of wind instruments. Their bold and brassy fanfares, falling upon the ear first from one direction then from another, proclaimed Venetian wealth and power as clearly as the gold and marble of the city's churches and palaces.

Monteverdi wrote some magnificent antiphonal music on his own account. He also wrote more operas, for in addition to the glories of St Mark's and the pomp and pageantry of the famous doges, Venice was also a centre of secular art and entertainment, and the first city to have a public opera house. Some of Monteverdi's opera scores are lost, but those which have survived have earned him recognition as the first truly great opera composer. He breathed emotion and passion into the monodies and RECITATIVES of the individual characters, contrasting these with duets and other vocal ensembles to add to the drama. Moreover, by exploiting the special sound qualities of the accompanying instruments, he created music that was much more varied in tone than that produced by the older consorts of viols or recorders. Today, our senses often swamped by sensations of every kind, it is difficult to realize just how sensational, in the true sense of the word, Monteverdi's operas must have been to those who first saw and heard them.

Opera quickly spread from Italy to other parts of Europe during the seventeenth century, notably to France where it was enthusiastically taken up by Louis XIV and his court. France was the most powerful European country during Louis's long reign, and as a symbol of this pre-eminence he had built at Versailles, not far from Paris, a magnificent palace set amongst ornamental gardens and lakes on the grandest scale. Known as *Le Roi Soleil* ('The Sun King'), Louis attracted to Versailles some of the most talented artists, writers and musicians of the age. Among them was Jean-Baptiste Lully, born in Italy but taken to France as a child. Lully was a ruthless man in some ways, securing for himself virtual control of all opera production in France, but he made good use of his position, creating a brilliant new style of opera. One important feature of this was the inclusion of ballet, since dancing played a large part in the social life at Versailles, and in several of Lully's opera-ballets there was a dancing role for the King himself. A second notable feature was the way Lully, who was a friend of the dramatists Corneille, Racine and Moliere, shaped his music to the manner of speech they had established in the French theatre. In addition, Lully established a form of *ouverture* (the French for 'opening' or 'beginning') to his operas, with a slow, stately opening, a faster middle section and a slow conclusion, which was to influence, at a later date, the development of the orchestral symphony.

The grandeur of buildings like the palace of Versailles, and of the opera-ballets staged there, is typical of one aspect of the artistic period called Baroque. This period also saw a great flowering of instrumental music. François Couperin, another of Louis XIV's musicians, wrote religious music for the Royal Chapel at Versailles, and was a fine organist; but he is best remembered today for his keyboard compositions. Couperin wrote most of his harpsichord music as groups of short pieces based mainly on court dances such as the GAVOTTE, MINUET and

Italian virginal, dated 1550. In Italy these are often called 'spinets', but in England 'spinet' describes a different type of keyboard instrument.

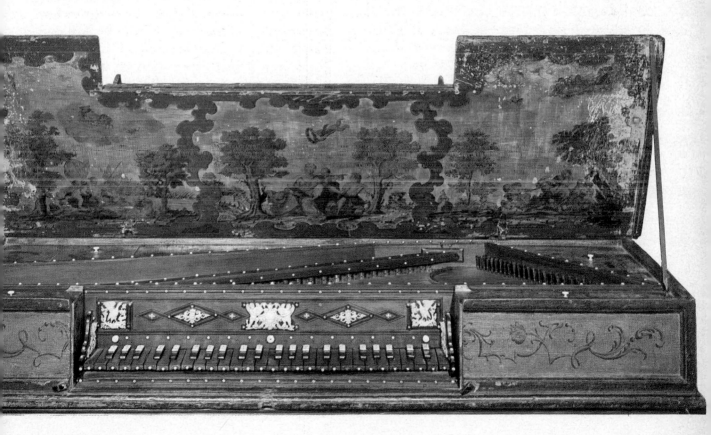

Young Woman Playing a Harpsichord by the seventeenth-century
Dutch painter Jan Steen. The boy coming down the stairs is
carrying a theorbo—a type of bass lute.

SARABANDE. These groups were originally published under the title of *ordres*, but we know them better as SUITES (another French word meaning 'what follows' in the sense of a succession of pieces). The form of the suite was used by many other Baroque composers, including J.S. Bach, the French names for the dances usually being retained. Couperin also gave descriptive titles to some of his pieces, such as *Les Petits Moulins a Vent* ('The Little Windmills'), probably to please the children at court who went to him for lessons. There is, however, a genuine connection between the image or idea suggested by the titles and the character of the music—something which Debussy and Ravel, two of the greatest composers of French piano music, later transformed into a kind of musical impressionism. Couperin also wrote a treatise on the technique of playing the harpsichord. This tells us a good deal more about the special way keyboard music was played in Couperin's own time than can be understood just by an examination of the printed music.

The seventeenth century also brought with it the big change from the viol family of bowed stringed instruments to the violin and its deeper-toned relatives. Violins began to be made in the sixteenth century. They produced a clearer, brighter tone than viols, but did not at first find much favour with musicians, who preferred the more subdued and dark sound of viols for their own polyphonic style of music. Gradually, though, people came to recognize in the violin qualities of tone and of agility which brought it closer to the human voice than any other instrument, and made it the best instrumental counterpart to the new vocal music of opera. This appreciation of the violin's special new qualities encouraged musicians to start thinking of it as a solo instrument. Viols were best played together in consort. The violin was at its best soaring off on its own, giving to much Baroque instrumental and orchestral music an exciting new sense of freedom and space.

Monteverdi experimented with violins, and at about the same time a famous instrumental ensemble, *Les vingt-quatre violons du Roy* ('The King's twenty-four violins'), was created at the French court. Charles II of England afterwards formed a similar ensemble when he returned from exile in France. Italy, though, was the real starting point in the history of the violin and its music. It was in the little north Italian town of Cremona that several families of craftsmen perfected violin construction. Antonio Stradivari is the best known of these craftsmen today, and the violins, violas and cellos made by him and his colleagues are now some of the most highly prized possessions in the world of music. Stradivari's almost exact contemporary, Arcangelo Corelli, was the first important composer of violin music. He also did more than anyone else to create a new type of instrumental composition, called the CONCERTO GROSSO. The

Antonio Vivaldi, one of the greatest Baroque composers for the violin.

Giuseppe Tartini, a great violinist who was also an important musical theorist and technician (see also page 164).

Italian word 'concerto' literally means the playing together of a group of instrumentalists. The concerto grosso, or 'great concerto', was in fact written for two groups of string players, a large group known as the *ripieno* ('full'), and a smaller group of soloists, the two bodies of sound being contrasted in alternating passages of the music.

Corelli worked for many years in Rome, in the service of a cardinal. Antonio Vivaldi, the other outstanding master of the Italian concerto grosso for string orchestra, spent most of his life in his native city of Venice as a teacher at a girls' orphanage. From his enormous output of music the most celebrated composition is the group of four concertos for strings and solo violin called *Le Quattro Stagioni* ('The Four Seasons'). The

music is most descriptive, Vivaldi himself indicating in the score such allusions to nature as bird song and storms. There is even a fall on the ice! In this respect the work was ahead of its time by nearly a hundred years, anticipating the instrumental PROGRAMME MUSIC of Romantic composers like Berlioz and Liszt. Vivaldi wrote expressive and passionate music for the strings and solo violins. He also composed concertos for other solo instruments including the trumpet, flute and bassoon, and was one of the first composers to write music for the clarinet which had recently been invented.

France and Italy were the two leading musical nations during the sixteenth and most of the seventeenth centuries. Germany, meanwhile, had been the principal battleground of the Thirty Years War, a bitter and confused conflict of power involving Catholics and Protestants, which also continued the stuggle between the Hapsburg and Bourbon royal dynasties. Long after the fighting was over large parts of Germany remained devastated, and the people subdued. Yet as far as music was concerned, the situation was soon to change, and for nearly two hundred years it would be the music of the German-speaking people that dominated all else.

The first two great German masters were Johann Sebastian Bach and George Frideric Handel. They were born in the same year, within a hundred miles of each other, but both the course of their lives and the character of their music were very different. Bach was a devoted family man, soon marrying again when his first wife died. He never travelled outside his own country, though his various court and church appointments kept him on the move. None of these brought him the rewards or the recognition he thought he deserved, but his three longest-held appointments are also important because they largely shaped the pattern of his creative life.

The first of these was as organist at the court of the Duke of Weimar. It was as an organist that Bach was most acclaimed in his own lifetime, and his love of the instrument remained

Portrait of Johann Sebastian Bach as a young man.

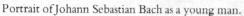

Detail of a magnificent Baroque church organ built by Gottfried Silbermann, a famous German instrument maker.

throughout his life. As a young man he once walked the best part of two hundred miles to hear the celebrated Danish organist-composer Dietrich Buxtehude perform at a church in the old Hanseatic Baltic port of Lübeck. Bach also had a detailed technical knowledge of the organ and was sometimes consulted on matters of construction and installation. His own organ compositions, many dating from his years at Weimar, are acknowledged by all to be the greatest for the instrument. Bach wrote many FANTASIAS, TOCCATAS, CHORALE-PRELUDES—composed around the theme of a Lutheran chorale—and PRELUDES and FUGUES. The fugue is one of the most highly developed forms of polyphony, more usually described as COUNTERPOINT. Some people are put off by the word 'fugue' and think that such music must be heavy and academic; but in Bach's hands a fugue, building itself up from the interplay of one or

35

more melodic lines, parts or 'voices', can achieve a strength and power that has no parallel in music.

Bach's next appointment was to the court of Prince Leopold of Anhalt-Cöthen, and here he wrote most of his instrumental and orchestral music, including the first part of his greatest keyboard work, *Das Wohltemperierte Clavier*. The title means 'The Well-tempered, or Well-tuned, Keyboard', and behind it lies a significant aspect of musical theory. As the old medieval church modes had been gradually replaced during the sixteenth and seventeenth centuries by the much more flexible harmonic arrangement of major and minor keys, so certain technical difficulties arose. One was the problem of how to tune keyboard instruments. If they were tuned with absolute accuracy of pitch in one scale, they would be out of tune by a greater or lesser degree in every other scale. The solution was to adjust or 'temper' the pitch relationships just enough to allow all the keys and scales to be played equally well. Bach was in favour of this idea of 'equal temperament' for keyboard instruments, and showed his support by writing one prelude and one fugue for such instruments in each of the twenty-four major and minor keys, as if to say, 'Look what the new tuning method allows me to do!' He later wrote another twenty-four such pieces, the complete set also being known as the 'Forty-Eight Preludes and Fugues'.

While with Prince Leopold, Bach also composed a group of six orchestral works which are a cross between a French suite and the Italian concerto grosso, each written for a different combination of instruments thus emphasizing the contrasting orchestral sounds. He hoped they might obtain him a job with the Count of Brandenburg. 'Your Highness took some pleasure in the insignificant talents which Heaven has given me for Music', Bach wrote to the Count referring to an earlier meeting between them. 'I have then, in accordance with Your Highness's most gracious orders, taken the liberty of rendering my most humble duty to Your Royal Highness with the present Concertos.' These 'Brandenburg' Concertos, that have given so much pleasure and joy to millions, were discovered years after the composer's death, neglected and unopened on a library shelf.

Bach's final appointment, only secured after other candidates had dropped out, was as cantor, or director of music, to the Church and School of St Thomas in Leipzig. There he wrote much of his choral music, many of the church cantatas, and the St John and St Matthew Passions. The 'Passion' is that part of the four New Testament gospels describing Christ's betrayal, trial and crucifixion. The intense drama of these events

Handsome 'double' flageolet. These woodwind instruments were similar to recorders and were popular up to the eighteenth century.

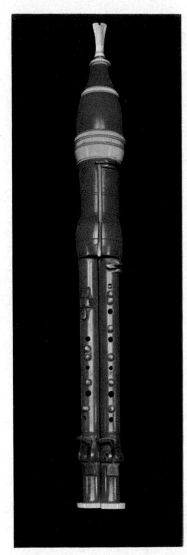

had inspired musical settings since the Middle Ages. Bach's own models were the Passions of an earlier German composer, Heinrich Schütz, who had studied with Giovanni Gabrieli in Venice and so learnt a dramatic way of writing for voices. The St John and St Matthew Passions contain solo parts for the main characters in the drama, including Pontius Pilate, Judas and Christ himself. They are set to Luther's German translation of the Bible and include some of the Lutheran chorales. Bach expressed his own deep religious faith in one other large-scale choral work, the Mass in B minor. This was another composition, now regarded as one of the highest peaks in the art of music, which Bach hoped might lead to new employment, a post with the Roman Catholic Elector of Saxony. However, as with the Brandenburg Concertos, he was disappointed.

Handel had his share of misfortune, but he was also much luckier than Bach. Moreover, his chosen field of music, opera, combined with his own robust and sociable personality, kept him in the limelight. Opera was the one branch of music that offered the prospect of large financial rewards to an eighteenth-century composer. Handel first joined an opera orchestra in Hamburg, then travelled to Italy, where he studied the instrumental music of Corelli and the operas of Alessandro Scarlatti, and had his own first operas produced with great success. He returned for a short while to his native land, to become director of music to the Elector of Hanover, but was soon off again, this time to the large and prosperous city of London. Twenty years earlier Henry Purcell's one true opera, *Dido and Aeneas*, had been staged, and it contained some of the most emotionally powerful music ever written by an Englishman. It had not, however, given rise to an English operatic style. Instead there was a growing interest in Italian opera, which Handel was well equipped to write. In about two weeks he composed a new Italian-style opera, *Rinaldo*, and had it accepted for production. The first performance, which apparently included the release of a flock of starlings above the stage, was a huge success and, for

George Frideric Handel, painted when he was thirty-six years old.

the time being at any rate, Handel was in a position of fame and prosperity. He settled in London and later became a British subject.

Handel's early years in England were helped in other ways. The Elector of Hanover, who was Handel's old employer, had been invited by the English parliament to become their king, and as George I of England he gave the composer valuable support. Handel also found a good patron in the Duke of Chandos. This gentleman was exceedingly wealthy and had built a large mansion called Canons near Edgware, just north of London. Handel lived on the duke's estate for three years and wrote for him a fine set of anthems and a type of English pastoral opera called *Acis and Galatea*. But his first interest remained opera for the London stage.

Christ and his mother Mary depicted in a German Renaissance painting. The life and person of Jesus Christ inspired three of the greatest Baroque choral works—Bach's two settings of the Passion and Handel's *Messiah*.

The Italian style of OPERA SERIA at which Handel excelled was noted particularly for its spectacle and for the exciting singing provided by castrato singers (eunuchs)—grown men who still sang like boys. The tradition of castrato singing was started centuries before by the Church, which did not permit women to take part in religious music. The choir of the Sistine Chapel in Rome was noted for its castrati, although during the seventeenth and eighteenth centuries many of them made their way into opera, to be treated like pop stars and paid enormous fees. On the other hand, this kind of Italian *opera seria* had very complicated plots, taken from mythology or ancient history, and was full of rigid conventions about how many arias should be given to each singer and when the singers should enter and leave the stage. Its popularity was probably already past its peak when an entirely new kind of stage entertainment, *The*

Beggar's Opera, with dialogue by John Gay and music based on popular English ballads, took London by storm. For a time Handel struggled on against this change of fortune, then suffered a stroke. Upon his recovery he turned his attention more to ORATORIO than to opera.

Oratorio takes its name from the kind of religious music performed in the Oratory of St Philip Neri in Rome during the sixteenth century. These performances developed as a kind of religious opera, but without stage settings, costumes or dramatic action. Bach's settings of the Passion were similar to oratorio. Handel set to music many different Bible stories in his oratorios, achieving his greatest success and most lasting fame in this field with *Messiah*. Not long after his death the English custom was established of giving performances of *Messiah* with a very large chorus and orchestra and in a mood of great piety. Modern performances usually return to the much smaller chorus and orchestra of Handel's own day, and are given at the brisker rate he himself would probably have directed. In this way—like old paintings that come up looking wonderfully bright after layers of varnish have been removed—they communicate the true exuberance of much Baroque art and music.

Bach and Handel lived well into the eighteenth century—the Age of Reason, as it is called—and their styles of music died with them. In place of the magnificence of polyphony and the grand manner of *opera seria*, which they exemplified, there emerged a lighter, more graceful style of music, called 'Rococo', or the *style galant*. A comparable change in the fine arts would be from the large, rather florid paintings of Peter Paul Rubens to the more fanciful, delicate pictures and decoration of an artist like Antoine Watteau. Another notable feature of eighteenth-century life, which reflected a new mood of toleration and relaxation, was the Grand Tour. The educated and well-to-do might travel around Europe for two or three years in a spirit of enlightened inquiry. Greece and Italy were the two countries they most wanted to see, marvelling at the beautiful form and proportion of such

Detail from a painting by the Italian artist Giambattista Tiepolo, showing two characters dancing a minuet. Many of Tiepolo's paintings, like those of Watteau, are typical of the Rococo style of art.

monuments to classical antiquity as the Parthenon in Athens. Indeed, artists, writers and musicians of this time, which became known as the Classical period, were inspired to create works which were carefully proportioned in imitation of the works of antiquity. The Classical style in music was that in which questions of proportion and balance were uppermost in the composer's mind.

The two musical forms most closely associated with these Classical aims and ideals were the SYMPHONY and the SONATA. Neither term was new. Many Renaissance pieces for groups of instruments were called symphonies, and the

Left: Christoph Willibald Gluck, an important composer of opera in the generation that followed Handel.
Below: Eighteenth-century spinet, handsomely decorated in the Rococo style.

name was sometimes given to an orchestral interlude in a larger choral work, such as the 'Pastoral' Symphony from Handel's *Messiah*. Sonata, from the Italian *suonare* ('to sound'), was the name given in the seventeenth century to pieces for small instrumental groups, as distinct from CANTATA (Italian *cantare* 'to sing'), describing a piece for voices. Corelli wrote many such pieces, calling them either *sonata da camera* ('sonata for the room') if they were intended for a social occasion, or *sonata da chiesa* if they were written for church performance. During the eighteenth century, however, the words 'symphony' and 'sonata' took on the meaning by which they are best understood today.

The symphony was an orchestral composition which originally grew out of the various kinds of operatic overture. These OVERTURES, or SINFONIAS as they were sometimes called, had contrasting fast and slow sections which attracted the new composers because of the sense of musical balance and proportion they created. The earliest eighteenth-century symphonies or sinfonias, therefore, were rather like extended overtures, and often described simply as 'grand overture'. Then, after the manner of the suite, they began to be written as a small group of individual pieces, or movements, with due consideration to matters of contrast and balance between the movements.

As composers explored these new ways of constructing orchestral music, so they became increasingly concerned with the way it should sound. Earlier Baroque orchestras had varied considerably in size and instrumental make-up depending on the availability of players. This situation did not unduly worry composers like Bach and Handel, who made frequent new arrangements of their own and other people's music; but it was not satisfactory for the performance of the new symphonies. To achieve the clear, well-defined quality of sound they required, the new generation of Classical composers became more selective over their use of instruments in the orchestra. They dropped altogether some of the instruments used by the older Baroque composers, and reorganized the

rest according to their particular qualities of sound and capabilities. The German court at Mannheim maintained one of the best orchestras in the eighteenth century. Here much pioneer work was done in the new art of writing symphonies. The technique of contrasting a soft orchestral passage for a few instruments with a passage for full orchestra (TUTTI), and the carefully controlled increase in orchestral sound from soft to loud (CRESCENDO), were two new features of orchestral music specially associated with the so-called Mannheim School.

Sonatas were composed along the same lines of musical thought as symphonies but were

Fine eighteenth-century portrait of a court flautist. The flute was a very popular instrument of the time, notably with Frederick the Great of Prussia (see also page 139).

written for one or two instruments only, or for a solo keyboard instrument. They also gave their name to a special new way of constructing a piece of music, which represents more completely than anything else the ideals and character of eighteenth-century Classical music. This was SONATA FORM, used as the basis for many individual movements in sonatas, symphonies, concertos and other compositions of the period. One of the origins of sonata form is to be found in the keyboard sonatas of Alessandro Scarlatti's son Domenico. In many of his one-movement keyboard sonatas Domenico Scarlatti started the music in one key, then TRANSPOSED (or 'changed') to another key and to a new tune, before returning to his opening ideas. This was called binary, or two-part form. Sonata form considerably extended this method of musical construction, dividing a piece of music into three main sections. These were the 'exposition', the 'development' and the 'recapitulation', and they were closely linked and balanced by changes of key and by changes in the musical ideas from one section to the next. Sonata form presented composers with a whole new set of rules; it also allowed them to concentrate more ideas into a single piece of music than had previously been possible. Moreover, with its contrasting themes, key changes and variations of mood, it gave them the opportunity of packing their music with a new dramatic punch and tension.

Johann Stamitz, musical director at the Court of Mannheim, and his son Karl were two early composers of the Classical symphony. Two of J.S. Bach's most gifted children, Carl Philipp Emanuel and Johann Christian Bach, were important figures in the development of Classical form and of newer styles in keyboard music. Nevertheless, the man who is considered to have perfected all these Classical forms was Franz Joseph Haydn. He was born into a humble peasant family in a village now on the borders of Austria and Hungary, but rose to become musical director at the Court of Esterházy in the Hungarian district of Galanta. There he wrote music as it was demanded of him, masses and

Franz Joseph Haydn during his years of service at the court of Esterházy.

other religious works, and operas for court entertainment. But his employer for many years, Prince Nikolaus Esterházy, was a cultured man who liked Haydn and gave him time to experiment with the new Classical styles of composition. The string quartet, consisting of two violins, viola and cello—a beautifully balanced combination of instruments—was a type of composition associated with Haydn above all other musicians. Haydn is also sometimes called the 'Father of the Symphony'. This is not strictly true, but he did more than any other single person to shape it into an orchestral work of four well contrasted movements, and so created the framework for some of the greatest music of the next hundred years. The symphony orchestra as we know it today, organized under the four instrumental headings of strings, woodwind, brass and percussion, also owes a great deal to Haydn's example.

The best known of his symphonies are the twelve he composed specially for his two visits to England when he was already a famous man. They are symphonies numbers 93 to 104, often called the 'Salomon Symphonies' after the London violinist and impresario J.P. Salomon who organized the visits. Some of them have nicknames alluding to a particular feature of the music. The Symphony number 94 is known as the 'Surprise' because of a loud chord that unexpectedly interrupts the quiet progress of the slow movement. 'That will make the ladies jump!' Haydn is supposed to have said of this famous chord. The nicknames, however, are not nearly as important as the fact that these symphonies of Haydn, like his string quartets, trios and sonatas, are beautifully ordered, balanced and controlled in the finest Classical manner of the eighteenth century. They are also the work of a brilliant and successful man who remained kindly and good humoured to the end of his days.

The other great composer of the Classical period was Wolfgang Amadeus Mozart. He is remembered as a child prodigy mainly because at the age of six his father Leopold took him and his little sister on a tour, performing in the courts of Europe, where he created a sensation. His first real job, as a court musician to the Archbishop of Salzburg, was not so glamorous. Mozart found Salzburg, his home town, a dull place after his travels, while he and his employer came to detest each other. The result was that Mozart lost his job, never obtaining another worthwhile post. He then decided to settle in Vienna and married, still confident of success. At first things did go well. He was in demand as composer, performer and teacher. Haydn, by then the most eminent musician in Europe, publicly said of Wolfgang to his father, 'I tell you before God and as an honest man, your son is the greatest composer whom I know personally or by repute'. Despite these prospects and glowing recommendations, Mozart and his wife Constanze could not man-

age their affairs. He ran up debts, she was often pregnant and ill, and soon he was begging for money. When he died his body was placed in a pauper's grave during a heavy storm and nobody could remember afterwards where it lay.

Mozart wrote over six hundred works, according to the catalogue compiled by Ludwig von Köchel, a scholar who listed them in their probable order of composition. Today they are invariably quoted with their 'K' number. Six hundred compositions may sound like a colossal output, especially for someone who died before he was forty, but it is not all that exceptional by eighteenth-century standards. Composers were called upon to write new music for each and every social or religious occasion, and in many cases such music was only performed once, then shelved and perhaps lost for ever or only discovered again years after the composer's death. Mozart turned out divertimentos, serenades, sets of dances, early symphonies, to every new commission, producing such music in the light Rococo style at great speed.

With a few exceptions, it is those works with a K number of around 400 and above, that contain Mozart's greatest music. These include the six string quartets he dedicated to his friend Haydn; the last group of piano concertos, which are remarkable for the way they contrast the solo instrument with the orchestra; and the last three symphonies, numbers 39, 40 and 41 (known as the 'Jupiter' Symphony). From a technical point of view many of these compositions contain passages that are astonishingly advanced in terms of harmony or the general shaping of their ideas. Written in an age of order and reason, they are no less remarkable for their sense of personal feeling. The fact that Mozart always composed with such a flawless control of Classical form makes the expressive quality of a work such as the Quintet in G minor all the more poignantly beautiful.

The beauty, the drama and moments even of passion in Mozart's greatest instrumental and orchestral work are like echoes of the music in his operas. It may indeed be said that Mozart was first and foremost an operatic composer and that

The child Mozart seated at the keyboard, his father Leopold and
sister Maria Anna, painted during their visit to Paris in 1764.

Vienna in the late eighteenth century when Mozart lived there.
The scene shows the Burg Theatre where some of his greatest
operas were first produced.

it is his music for the theatre that spilled over into
everything else he wrote. A little earlier in the
century another important composer of operas,
Christoph Willibald Gluck, condemned the
many conventions that had crept into opera over
the years, making it in his view a rather super-
ficial entertainment. He wanted opera to be
taken much more seriously, and for the music to
be closely linked to the dramatic action. In many
respects Mozart's operas are quite different from
those of Gluck, but they realize to a marvellous
degree that relationship between music and stage
action which the older composer desired.

Mozart's most fruitful operatic collaboration
was with the Italian poet and librettist Lorenzo
da Ponte. The latter's experience and feeling for
the stage raised Mozart's own inspiration to its
highest point. The first opera they created together (though by no means the first that Mozart
had written) was *Le Nozze di Figaro* ('The
Marriage of Figaro'). This is in the style of Italian
OPERA BUFFA, or comic opera, and there are some
very funny moments in the work. But the opera
as a whole has far more to it than comedy. It is

Papageno the Birdcatcher, one of the extraordinary characters in
Mozart's opera *The Magic Flute*. His librettist, Emanuel
Schikaneder, was a well-known Viennese actor and played the
part in the first production. The opera is in the style of *Singspiel*
('song-play') which has spoken dialogue in German instead of
sung recitative in the traditional Italian.

really about the relationship between an aristocratic master and his manservant Figaro. The
original play by the French dramatist Pierre
Beaumarchais had earlier been banned in France
because of its alleged attack on the aristocratic
system. In his libretto, da Ponte played down the
politics to some extent, but he still brought a
degree of social realism to the opera house that
was quite revolutionary for 1786. Beyond that,
Mozart's succession of arias and vocal ensembles
convey real human feelings, of great sadness as

well as happiness, in a way that no previous music had done. And he matched the high points in the stage action with music that is in no way limited by the normal operatic conventions of aria and recitative.

Early audiences could not have realized what a stupendous landmark in the history of opera *Le Nozze di Figaro* would turn out to be. Nevertheless, it was an immediate success, especially in Prague where it was staged soon after its Viennese première. In the event Mozart made very little money out of it (with no copyright laws to protect his music and guarantee an income), but he and da Ponte did secure a commission for another opera, and quickly set to work. This was based on the character of the legendary lover Don Juan. *Don Giovanni*, as they called their new opera, also has some comedy, but this is almost incidental to the main point of the story, which is that those who defy all moral laws bring about their own destruction. The dramatic intensity of the music that Mozart wrote for the closing scene, when Don Giovanni is finally dragged down to hell, has lost none of its power over the years. It is, in fact, first heard right at the beginning of the overture, thus casting a menacing shadow across the whole course of the action—a musically dramatic device used by many later composers.

Die Zauberflöte ('The Magic Flute') is a completely different kind of opera. Mozart wrote the music to a German libretto, and the work has spoken dialogue between arias instead of the Italian sung recitative. This style was very popular with the Viennese, as used in puppet shows or a type of pantomime. *Die Zauberflöte* opens almost like pantomime, with such fanciful characters as Papageno the Birdcatcher and the Queen of the Night. But it goes on to present much of the ritual of Freemasonry. Both Mozart and his new librettist Emanuel Johann Schikaneder were Freemasons (an ancient and semi-secret society that was constantly under attack from the church), and the composer wrote some beautifully solemn and moving music to those scenes expressing masonic ideals about the nobility and the brotherhood of man. He died soon after, in a

society still based firmly on social privilege; but in Paris the French Revolution, with its own ideas about equality and brotherhood, had begun.

Ludwig van Beethoven lived right through the period of the French Revolution and the Napoleonic Wars that followed. The Revolution itself fired the imagination of young artists and intellectuals like Beethoven, with its creed of *liberté*, *egalité*, *fraternité* ('liberty, equality, brotherhood'); the wars that came after destroyed the settled order of eighteenth-century life and its system of aristocratic patronage, making it necessary for Beethoven and those like him to lead more independent lives. Earlier examples can be found of artists and composers who chose, or were forced by circumstances, to try and make their own way in the world, but they were the exception rather than the rule. The vast majority of artists worked for the church or for the aristocracy. From Beethoven's time onwards, freedom and independence became the great watch-

Ludwig van Beethoven. The prefix 'van' indicates that his family were of Flemish or Dutch descent.

words in the world of the arts, while the image of Beethoven himself, with his huge shaggy head and brooding expression, stood for the artist as someone set apart from the rest of mankind.

Beethoven was born in the small Rhineland town of Bonn (now the capital of the German Federal Republic) and settled permanently in Vienna as a young man, apparently assured of his future as a brilliant pianist-composer. From the start he was a rebellious and radically-minded individual. He had patrons, rich Viennese aristocrats who recognized his genius and gave him generous support, but he was never an employee earning a regular salary and his relationship with them was quite different from that which existed forty or fifty years earlier between, for example, Haydn and Prince Esterházy. He regarded himself as their equal, and sometimes even insulted them with his remarks about the 'Princely Rabble'. But apart from his attitudes and opinions, what really dictated the pattern of Beethoven's life was his deafness, which began to trouble him at about the age of thirty and grew steadily worse from that time onwards. This ruined his career as a pianist, and though he continued sometimes to try and direct performances of his own music, the results were pitiful. Thus he was driven in upon himself and his genius, becoming the first musician of real greatness to concentrate almost entirely on composition.

The revolutionary spirit that Beethoven displayed as a man fills his music. He used his art to express personal beliefs in a way that no previous artist had done. His opera *Fidelio* is about political tyranny and the right of men to freedom of speech. His 'Choral' Symphony sets to music a poem by the German dramatist Johann Schiller proclaiming that men and women everywhere should look upon each other as brothers and sisters, equal and free. At a time when ideas about social and political democracy were only just beginning to be understood, these were thrilling sentiments indeed. Beyond such specific declarations of personal faith, Beethoven saw it as his mission to broaden the expressive power of music and so lead men and women to discover their own finest thoughts and feelings. The fact that he only gave OPUS numbers to those works or groups of works which he, not his publisher, considered important, witholding such numbers from others, shows how seriously he took his role as artist and composer. Today these opus numbers are a great help in the fascinating job of tracing the growth and development of Beethoven's ideas from one major composition to the next.

Such exalted artistic aims presented Beethoven with enormous technical problems of form and style. He probably never could have composed with the speed and facility of Mozart, nor with the steady assurance of Bach. In the event, composition for him was often a long, hard struggle. From the evidence of his sketch books we know he noted down ideas, then revised them over and over again until at last they expressed what he desired and were ready to fit into the larger framework of a composition. The end result of such hard, sometimes agonized methods of work is never comfortable, easy music. There are, indeed, some passages of Beethoven that sound almost awkward, as though he were literally hammering his way through to the solution of some great problem or to the realization of some great musical scheme. But it is always music of tremendous concentration and power.

The nine symphonies are Beethoven's most celebrated group of works. In them he built up the symphony into the most elevated type of orchestral composition, and set the standard by which nearly all later composers of symphonies have been judged. The fact that he wrote only nine, compared with the number produced by Haydn and Mozart, is in itself an indication of the time and effort he put into their composition. The Third Symphony in E flat major ('Eroica', opus 55) is one of the towering landmarks of Western music for the way that it advances the frontiers of music in so many new directions at once, in terms of form, style, size and power of feeling. Beethoven had planned to dedicate this symphony to Napoleon, but struck the dedication from the title page of the manuscript

Napoleon inspecting his troops. When he bombarded Vienna in 1809, Beethoven had to shelter in a cellar and protect his ears with pillows since loud noises affected his already damaged hearing.

when he heard that Napoleon had had himself crowned Emperor of the French. To the composer the taking of a crown was a betrayal of the Revolution. The Fifth Symphony in C minor (opus 67) has an opening movement of unprecedented musical concentration and force. Beethoven also links the third and fourth movements by an extraordinary passage that sounds as though the music is plunging down into a long, dark tunnel, finally to emerge in a triumphant blaze. The Sixth Symphony ('Pastoral', opus 68) is the first symphony to have a descriptive 'programme', evoking Beethoven's deep love of the countryside. The Ninth Symphony in D minor ('Choral', opus 125) crowns the series when soloists and chorus join the orchestra in the closing 'Ode to Joy'.

The two other most substantial groups of Beethoven's compositions are the thirty-two piano sonatas and (as originally written) sixteen string quartets. The piano was Beethoven's favourite instrument, and despite his deafness he continued to take an interest in the improvements in piano construction and design that took place during his lifetime. His sonatas explore the piano's growing possibilities to the full. The huge Sonata in B flat major (opus 106), known as the 'Hammerklavier' Sonata, remains to this day the severest test of a pianist's abilities and stamina, and must have been virtually unplayable on any instrument of Beethoven's time. It was written towards the end of his life, when he was cut off from normal contact with the world of sound and absorbed with ever more complex problems of form and style.

Another fearsome test of the players' abilities is the last movement that Beethoven originally wrote to his String Quartet, also in B flat major

Viennese musicians playing in a tavern at about the time of
Beethoven and Schubert.

(opus 130). This, like the last movement of the
'Hammerklavier' Sonata, takes the basic form
of a gigantic fugue. Beethoven's publishers,
alarmed at the piece, persuaded him to substitute
a much easier final movement to the quartet, and
published the original separately as the *Grosse
Fuge* ('Great Fugue', opus 133). For a long time
this was usually played by a full string orchestra,
as the music was considered much too demand-
ing for just four players to cope with.

By the last years of his life Beethoven was
famous and revered, and might well have relaxed
his efforts, but he continued to reach out in new
creative directions with his massive and puzzling

compositions. He also had to struggle against
chronic ill health, including a kind of dropsy, or
swelling of the abdomen. The doctors who were
called to his lodgings, where he lived alone and in
depressing squalor, tried to relieve the symptoms
by drawing a watery fluid from his stomach.
'Better from my belly than from my pen' the
composer is reported to have said, defiant to the
last.

Beethoven was one of the key figures in the big
change from the eighteenth-century Classical
period to the nineteenth-century Romantic artistic movement. The Romantic artist, whether
he was a painter, writer or musician, was far

Franz Schubert. He had some devoted friends but was virtually unknown as a composer for years after his death.

such Romantic poets as William Wordsworth, symbolizing their own free creative spirits.

Romantic music reached an early peak of brilliance in the years immediately after Beethoven's death. Franz Schubert, who lived for only another year after Beethoven, wrote symphonies, string quartets and quintets and piano sonatas that contain some magnificent music, but his major contribution to the Romantic movement lies with his songs, or *Lieder* to give them their familiar German name. These are all settings of existing poems. A memorable feature of many of them is the striking piano part that accompanies the singer, creating the mood of the song as vividly as the scenery or lighting on a stage. One famous example is *Der Erlkönig* ('The Erl King'), to words by Johann Wolfgang von Goethe, in which the piano part most graphically suggests the headlong flight on horseback, through a dark and stormy night, of a father and his sick child, pursued by the Erl King or Elf King, dread harbinger of death. Later Schubert wrote two major song-cycles, or groups of songs linked by a common theme. They are *Die Schöne Müllerin* ('The Fair Maid of the Mill') and *Die Winterreise* ('The Winter Journey'), in both of which unrequited love and bitterness of heart are set against the natural world of woods and streams, sun, wind and snow. Indeed, so great were Schubert's achievements in this field that he virtually created in his *Lieder* a new musical art form, and after him came a distinguished line of other *Lieder* composers.

more concerned than his eighteenth-century predecessors with the free expression of feelings and ideas, usually attaching greater importance to the content of his work than to the form it might take. Romantic composers wrote music that was by turns very dramatic and tempestuous, joyful, sad or dreamily poetic in mood. They were also inspired by the work of great dramatic poets like Dante, Shakespeare and Goethe, producing music that was far more descriptive of certain moods, places or events than any written in earlier centuries. Nature, too, wild and untouched by the hand of man, appealed strongly to some of them, as it did to

The piano, beloved of Beethoven, was taken up with enthusiasm by several of the greatest Romantic composers. The improvisatory style favoured by the Viennese musicians had been employed by Beethoven himself in such pieces as the first movement of his so-called 'Moonlight' Sonata, and by Schubert in some of his groups of short piano pieces. This made it sound as though the composer had just sat down at the piano and started playing. Robert Schumann developed this style of piano music further, writing several groups of pieces which convey with true Romantic ardour the idea of spontaneous inspiration and self-discovery. In his piano music

A dramatic painting of the Erl King—the spectre of death—the subject of one of Schubert's greatest songs.

Frédéric Chopin by the French painter Eugène Delacroix—the portrait of one great Romantic artist by another.

particularly, Schumann was a typical Romantic in that he related it also to events in his private life. He often took the names of people or places close to his heart and cleverly applied the letters of the name in question to the corresponding notes on the piano. This way of linking letters with musical notes held a special appeal for him, since he was almost as interested in literature as he was in music. The piano meant even more to Frédéric Chopin. He was born in Poland, and although he spent most of his adult life in France, he felt constantly drawn towards the country of his birth. Due to its geographical position, Poland had for centuries been a battleground for other nations, and there were times when the country disappeared completely from the map. Chopin expressed his love and sympathy for the downtrodden Polish people in a group of stirring POLONAISES (the French word for a type of Polish dance) and in a much larger group of pieces based on another traditional Polish dance called the MAZURKA. These, and almost everything else he wrote, were compositions for the solo piano. Much of this music has a strong, impulsive, or dreamily Romantic sound to it. In reality, Chopin was a fastidious composer who thought very hard about every note he put down, and because of this attention to detail his music combines Romantic feeling with an almost Classical refinement.

Hector Berlioz, by contrast, was as much a figure of Romanticism in his person as in his music—a passionate and headstrong young man. 'Mad Hector of the Flaming Locks' people called him on account of his thick, reddish hair. He was a struggling young musician in Paris in 1830, at a time when the city was already a centre of Romantic art and literature and in the throes of another revolution caused by the restoration of the monarchy after the Napoleonic Wars. In this colourful and turbulent atmosphere, Berlioz fell desperately in love with a young Shakespearian actress from Ireland named Harriet Smithson, and composed his *Symphonie Fantastique*. The movements of this symphony evoke the feverish dreams of a lovesick young

Top: Contemporary cartoon of Berlioz conducting a huge orchestra and artillery! *Above:* Liszt depicted as a true wizard of the keyboard. Such pictures humorously point up the wilder side of Romantic music.

artist (in effect the composer himself), proceeding from a phantom ballroom to a march to the scaffold and a final witches' dance. For these wild and lurid scenes Berlioz wrote music that blazes with orchestral 'colour'. He was one of the most original masters of Romantic orchestral music, producing tonal effects from the instruments very much as though he were painting pictures in sound.

One of the most remarkable figures in the whole period of Romantic music was Franz Liszt. From the days of his youth when he looked like a Greek god to his venerable old age, he occupied the very centre of the nineteenth-century musical stage. Born in Hungary, Liszt achieved early fame as the outstanding figure among the first generation of true VIRTUOSO pianists—those who exploited the growing strength and power of the piano to show off their technical wizardry and physical stamina. In this capacity he may have been the first to adopt the practice of placing the instrument sideways on the platform so that the sound could most effectively be projected at the audience when the lid was raised, though cynics said it was to give them the benefit of his beautiful profile! Whatever the case, Liszt was a phenomenal success wherever he went. There are drawings of women fainting in his presence, and cartoons which show pianos collapsing beneath his assault. Much of the music Liszt wrote and played as a virtuoso pianist, however, was of little real merit, and as a truly creative artist he tired of the life. He then settled for some years in Weimar, where J.S. Bach had worked before him, devoting himself to serious composition and giving much help and encouragement to colleagues.

In several of his piano works Liszt made important advances in musical form and structure. For the orchestra he developed PROGRAMME MUSIC to the full—music intended to describe particular events, places and moods—creating a type of composition which he called a SYMPHONIC POEM. Another major work of programme music is the 'Faust' Symphony for chorus and orchestra, inspired by Goethe's poetic drama about the scholar Faust and his pact

Above: Felix Mendelssohn, brilliant, famous and rich. He was adored in Victorian England.
Left: Niccolò Paganini, whose feats of virtuosity on the violin equalled those of Liszt on the piano (see also page 152).

with the Devil, or Mephistopheles, in return for knowledge and power. This legend, with its basic theme of man challenging the dark forces of the supernatural, haunted the imagination of Romantic composers.

In the course of his career Liszt also made many piano TRANSCRIPTIONS of other composers' orchestral or operatic music. Some of these were merely virtuoso showpieces. Others were of greater value. As a work of true scholarship he transcribed the Beethoven symphonies for the piano. In the days before radio and the gramophone he thus brought great music into the homes of thousands who would probably have had no other chance to hear it.

The Romantic movement was not one continuous or headlong process of making music more descriptive, more colourful, or extrava-

gant. There were composers who could create a Romantic-sounding mood in their music while remaining quite conservative with regard to general matters of musical form and style. Felix Mendelssohn was such a man. At the age of only seventeen, while Beethoven still lived, he wrote his overture to Shakespeare's play *A Midsummer Night's Dream*. It is a masterpiece of Romantic orchestral music in the way it conjures up a mood of hushed, moonlit enchantment. Mendelssohn composed other fine pieces of descriptive music, including his overture 'Fingal's Cave' (the 'Hebrides' Overture), inspired by a visit he made to the Western Isles of Scotland. But he had a neat and orderly mind, and wrote much more music in the tried and tested forms of symphonies, concertos, string quartets, even preludes and fugues.

Mendelssohn was also famous in his own life-

time as a conductor. The art of conducting grew up during the nineteenth century. In earlier times composers usually took part in performances of their own music, giving a lead to the other players from their own place at a keyboard instrument or the front row of the violins. But with the appearance of works like the Beethoven symphonies orchestras grew larger and the music they had to play demanded more of them. Hence there was a need for someone to study the whole score of a piece, not just their own individual part, then lead the orchestra through detailed rehearsals and direct performances from a central rostrum where they could be seen clearly by all.

The arrival on the musical scene of the con-

Light-hearted nineteenth-century print of a ballroom scene. The waltz and the polka were the two favourite dances. Brahms loved the waltzes of Johann Strauss the Younger and wrote a group of his own for the piano.

ductor was part of the changing pattern of concert life. In the eighteenth century and before, orchestras were privately maintained by rich aristocrats, or they were simply a group of musicians recruited for a particular performance. In the nineteenth century the court orchestras of the aristocracy all but disappeared. The Industrial Revolution had brought a rapid increase in the size of towns and cities and produced a new generation of businessmen and tradespeople, who introduced their commercial ideas into music. Orchestras then started to be run like other businesses, maintained partly by private subscriptions, partly by receipts from public concerts. They needed conductors to help them build up a varied and interesting repertory, and a good conductor became an added attraction. Mendelssohn was principal conductor of the Leipzig Gewandhaus orchestra, one of the earliest permanent orchestras to be formed, and he did much both to popularize concert-going among the middle classes of the new industrial towns and cities (he was a great success in London and Birmingham as well as Germany) and to raise orchestral standards.

Mendelssohn had a deep respect for the music of earlier composers, and helped to bring Bach's music, long neglected, to a wider public. Johannes Brahms was equally impressed by the work of his predecessors, and of Beethoven in particular. Like Beethoven, he regarded composition as a very serious matter, and was extremely self-critical, destroying at least as much of his music as he allowed to be published. Brahms was especially cautious when it came to writing a symphony, feeling that Beethoven's achievements placed a heavy responsibility upon him. 'You don't know what it feels like to be dogged by that giant,' he wrote to a friend, while working on his First Symphony. This is in C minor, the key of Beethoven's Fifth Symphony, and shares with that work the same epic features, moving from a stormy and dramatic opening to a triumphant-sounding close. Brahms was evidently relieved to have his First Symphony behind him, and composed his remaining three symphonies with far greater ease. They are works of his full maturity, combining his great gifts for making musical ideas grow and change in true symphonic style with the Romantic qualities he knew well from Schumann's four symphonies written earlier in the century.

Brahms wrote other big works for the concert hall, including *Ein deutsches Requiem* (A German Requiem), a deeply moving choral and orchestral setting of passages from the Lutheran Bible

Cartoon of Brahms in old age, on the way to his favourite Viennese café, the 'Red Hedgehog'.

prompted by the death of his mother. Most of his output, however, is made up of *Lieder*, of sonatas and pieces for solo piano and chamber music written for many different instrumental groups. From the rather high-minded character of his early compositions, these works progress to the wonderfully rich and mellow mood of his later years.

Brahms's great German contemporary was Richard Wagner. The two men had a healthy respect for each other, but found themselves at the centre of a big musical and artistic controversy. The breathtaking speed with which

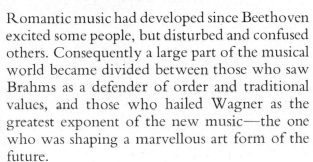

Above: Richard Wagner at about the age of fifty.
Right: The ghostly form of the Flying Dutchman's ship looms up out of the mist and darkness in Wagner's opera. The composer's own experience of a storm at sea may have inspired him to write the work.

Romantic music had developed since Beethoven excited some people, but disturbed and confused others. Consequently a large part of the musical world became divided between those who saw Brahms as a defender of order and traditional values, and those who hailed Wagner as the greatest exponent of the new music—the one who was shaping a marvellous art form of the future.

Wagner indeed believed this, and claimed also the right to be treated as an exceptional human being. He also prepared himself and the world for the wonderful things he planned to do in many books and articles containing all his ideas and theories. Inspired by the type of German Romantic opera which Carl Maria von Weber had already established, Wagner's aim from the start was to build up opera, musically and dramatically, into the greatest form of artistic expression. Weber's most successful opera, *Der Freischütz* ('The Marksman'), is patriotic in spirit, with its scenes of traditional German country life. Its plot concerns a pact with the Devil, made in a dreadful place called the Wolf's

Glen, and the eerie, terrifying mood music connected with this scene is a landmark in Romantic opera.

Significantly, Wagner's early opera *Der Fliegende Holländer* ('The Flying Dutchman') is also about the supernatural. But even at this early stage in his creative thinking, Wagner was concerned with more than just an exciting story. His characters stand for states of mind and spiritual values beyond their actual stage existence and thereby give the opera a new kind of depth and dimension. In *Tannhäuser* and *Lohengrin* which followed, Wagner similarly invested their themes of medieval pageantry with ideas about the conflict between sensual and spiritual love and redemption through love. He also wrote for them music of greater power and dramatic scope than any yet heard in an opera house.

Although in these relatively early operas Wagner was moving steadily towards his idea of a new art form, he realized how far he still had to go to achieve his aims. Yet he held steadfastly to his revolutionary vision of what he called 'music drama', and over a period of no less than twenty-five years finally completed what is probably the most ambitious and far-reaching work of art ever produced by one man. This is *Der Ring des Nibelungen* ('The Ring of the Nibelungs'), a gigantic cycle of four individual operas—*Das Rheingold* ('The Rhinegold'), *Die Walküre* ('The Valkyrie'), *Siegfried* and *Götterdämmerung* ('Twilight of the Gods'). The entire work is taken from Norse and Teutonic mythology, and based on a libretto that Wagner wrote out completely before starting the task of composition. Each opera in the cycle continues the saga of how a rock of gold is stolen from the Rhine and forged into a magic ring, of how this ring bears a terrible curse and so brings death and destruction to gods and men, until it is restored to its resting place deep beneath the waters of the river Rhine. At a deeper level this saga is about power and corruption and the world's salvation.

The music for 'The Ring' contains no conventional arias. It is almost entirely composed from motto themes which Wagner called *Leit-motiven* ('leading motives'). Beethoven in his Fifth Symphony had been among the first to use a 'motto theme' to bring special unity to a large composition. Berlioz, among other Romantic composers, also used a type of motto theme which he called an *idée fixe* ('fixed idea'). In 'The Ring' there are leading motives for every character, object or idea in the unfolding drama. One of them, for example, forms the tune of the the famous 'Ride of the Valkyrie'. These leading motives are laid out like a carpet of sound, over which the words of the drama are declaimed and the action proceeds. They accompany what is actually being sung and acted, they maintain an unbroken thread of musical and dramatic thought, and they signify the deeper symbolism of the drama, which was very important to Wagner.

The famous 'Ride of the Valkyries' in *The Ring of the Nibelungs*. The Valkyries bear the bodies of fallen warriors to their heavenly resting place in Valhalla.

Tristan and Isolde, two characters from Celtic legend who inspired another of Wagner's greatest music dramas.

Together with his use of *Leitmotiven*, Wagner took giant strides forward in writing for the orchestra. He did not change the way in which the Classical orchestra was arranged into strings, woodwind, brass and percussion, but continued the process, already well under way with Beethoven, of enlargement in all departments. He invented one new instrument, the Wagner tuba (actually more like a horn), and included some novel sound effects, such as the rhythm of anvils in *Das Rheingold* and steerhorns in *Götterdämmerung*. The very large orchestra needed for 'The Ring' is capable of delivering a massive volume of sound, but Wagner did not employ it just for that purpose. What he desired primarily was a rich and glowing quality of sound, and his

59

achievements here mark him as one of the greatest masters of orchestration.

There came a point in his creation of 'The Ring' when even Wagner's energy and confidence temporarily deserted him and he laid it aside. Very soon, however, he had begun two of his other greatest works. The passionate music written for the Celtic love story *Tristan und Isolde* ('Tristan and Isolde') is overwhelming. Wagner himself said that he composed the music in a kind of trance, as though powers beyond himself had taken possession of the work. The opera is remarkable for another aspect of Wagner's style, called 'chromaticism'. This has to do with harmony, and the way in which composers could modulate, or change key within a piece of music. The rules said that any piece of music, however much it might modulate, must be based on one particular key, and begin and end in that key. In *Tristan und Isolde*, Wagner's music modulates so much, starting from the very opening chords of the Prelude, that it is virtually free of any particular key. This was a harmonic revolution, leading to the ATONAL MUSIC (music without a normal tonal or key centre) created by many twentieth-century composers.

Die Meistersinger von Nürnberg ('The Mastersingers of Nuremberg'), the other opera Wagner composed before returning to his work on 'The Ring', is set in Renaissance Nuremberg, when the city was noted for the pageantry of its trades guilds and for its college of musicians, the Mastersingers themselves. It is called a comedy but the opera has more to do with politics. Wagner, a patriotic German, rejoiced in the political unification of his country under Bismarck's leadership, and *Die Meistersinger von Nürnberg* is a kind of hymn to German art and culture.

These operas, huge in scale and huge also in the demands they made on orchestra, singers and audiences alike, were not the end of Wagner's ambitions. He had built, to his own designs, in the small Bavarian town of Bayreuth, a *Festspielhaus*, or Festival Theatre, for the performance of his works. The man who provided much of the money for this project was Ludwig II of Bavaria,

one of many who had already fallen completely under the spell of the composer and his music. In 1876 'The Ring' was given its first complete performance there. As Wagner directed, the auditorium was darkened, there was no applause during the actual performance, and the sound of the orchestra came flooding up out of the darkness from an area below the stage. Against enormous odds he had achieved everything he set out to do, and made his music drama almost into a religion.

Ludwig of Bavaria was a very unbalanced man and was later declared insane, but in his feelings of adoration towards Wagner he was certainly not alone. Some of the most gifted men and women of the age idolized the composer, and his influence on all the arts, and on philosophy, was immense. In the German-speaking countries a whole generation of composers are often spoken

Anton Bruckner, in himself a quiet, simple man, but his symphonies are filled with grandeur.

of as the Post-Wagnerians—those coming after Wagner—chief among them being Anton Bruckner, Gustav Mahler and Richard Strauss. These three men were quite different from each other as people and as composers. Bruckner was a devout Catholic whose symphonies remind many people of the majestic columns, arches and stained glass of some great cathedral. Mahler was a deeply disturbed and nervous man who poured into his symphonies all his anxieties and spiritual conflicts. Strauss was much more a man of the world, who rose swiftly to fame and prosperity with a series of brilliantly orchestrated symphonic poems. But they each worked in the shadow of Wagner, and composed nearly all their music for a very large Wagnerian type of orchestra. At the beginning of the nineteenth century, orchestras seldom had more than thirty-five players. Towards the end of the century Bruckner, Mahler and above all Strauss

were writing for an orchestra of often more than a hundred musicians. And their music, whether they were writing symphonies, symphonic poems or operas, tended to be correspondingly long, weighty or complex, as though Wagner was never far from their thoughts.

Purely in the realm of opera, however, Wagner was not the only towering figure of his time. There was also Giuseppe Verdi in Italy. This was the country where opera had started. The Italians, with their great love of singing had developed a special style called BEL CANTO ('beautiful song'), which required vocal agility and a clear, pure tone of voice. Earlier in the century Gioacchino Rossini, Vincenzo Bellini and Gaetano Donizetti had written operas containing splendid tunes, with embellishments which were designed to give singers plenty of chances to show off these qualities and so win the hearts of every Italian audience. Verdi followed

Vincenzo Bellini, master of the *bel canto* operatic style.

Gioacchino Rossini, considered a very noisy composer in his own lifetime.

French print of a scene from *William Tell* which Rossini wrote specially for the Paris opera.

Giuseppe Verdi, composer and national hero, at the height of his fame.

in this tradition. He wrote music which his audiences would immediately understand and enjoy, adding a gift for strong, vigorous melody that sprang naturally from his peasant background. Indeed, people who never went near an opera house still knew many of his tunes as they rang out, loud and clear, from every street-corner barrel organ in Europe and America. As for the operas themselves, Verdi was not concerned with the deeper philosophical or spiritual ideas that so preoccupied Wagner. Good dramatic situations were what mattered to him, and once he was satisfied on that account he could bring to operatic life with equal success a victorious procession in ancient Egypt (*Aida*) or private grief in a nineteenth-century Paris drawing room (*La Traviata*) so that his audience was completely absorbed.

Verdi's first opera was produced when he was twenty-five, and with only a few interruptions he maintained a steady output over the years, each opera showing some musical or dramatic advance, as he gained in confidence and experience. Quite soon he was hailed as Italy's greatest composer, though some of his operas were failures when first produced. *Rigoletto*, the tragedy of a hunchbacked court jester, was one that made him internationally famous, and brought together some of his finest musical and dramatic ideas. Included in it is perhaps the best-

The gloomy dungeon tower where Manrico, 'The Troubadour', is imprisoned in Verdi's *Il Trovatore*.

known of all operatic arias, 'La donna è mobile' ('Woman is fickle').

Verdi was sixty when he composed *Aida*, which is one of the grandest of all operas, originally intended to celebrate the opening of the Suez Canal in 1869, though the production was not ready in time. He was eighty when he finished work on *Falstaff*, his great comic opera based on the Shakespearian character Sir John Falstaff, and the triumphant première took place at La Scala, Milan, in 1893. In that same year, not very far away in Turin, there was the première of Giacomo Puccini's first important opera *Manon Lescaut*, and it was almost as though the torch of Italian opera had been handed directly from the older composer to the younger. Puccini's famous arias are generally longer and more flowing than those written by Verdi; they often begin on a series of repeated notes, then rise and fall by intervals which are perfectly tailored to the human voice, finally soaring away into the highest flights of song. 'Che gelida manina' ('Your tiny hand is frozen') from *La Bohème* is a well-loved and fine example of Puccini's gift for melody.

These beautiful arias are only one side to Puccini's art. He also paid great attention to orchestration, using the orchestra, as Wagner did, to provide a kind of running commentary on all that is happening on stage. Some of the finest passages from his operas, in fact, are for the

An equally famous scene from Italian opera: Christmas Eve in the old Latin Quarter of Paris, the setting for Puccini's *La Bohème*.

orchestra alone, and Puccini used his fastidious ear for detail when writing such music to evoke a particular mood. For example, the last act of *Tosca* opens just before sunrise with the bells of all the churches in Rome chiming the hour, and Puccini went to a great deal of trouble to make sure that he wrote into his score the correct pitch and sequence of the bells in question. Two of his other operas, *Madame Butterfly* (the tragic story of a little Japanese geisha girl) and *Turandot* (about a legendary Chinese princess), are the result of Puccini's fascination with oriental subjects and musical styles. The art, ideas and music of the East appealed to others of his generation, notably Debussy, and have continued to influence other composers, such as Britten, Messiaen and Stockhausen, up to the present day.

Puccini also contributed to a style of opera called, in Italian, *verismo* meaning 'realistic'. This grew out of the work of French writers like Émile Zola and Guy de Maupassant who considered that literature and art in general, to be really truthful and honest, must be concerned with things that were ugly, diseased or brutal as well as subjects that were beautiful or ennobling in some way. Puccini's opera *Il Tabarro* ('The Cloak'), dealing with murder on a canal barge, is in the *verismo* tradition. Two other famous Italian operas of the period, *Cavalleria Rusticana* ('Rustic Chivalry') by Pietro Mascagni, and *I Pagliacci* ('The Clowns') by Ruggiero Leoncavallo, also owe something to this distinctive style of opera which brought scenes of a different side of life into the theatre.

The glittering auditorium of La Scala, Milan, the world's most famous opera house. Many other opera houses are modelled on its design.

Verdi was a national hero in politics as well as music. He lived during the period of the *Risorgimento*, the movement which liberated the north Italian provinces from the Austro-Hungarian Empire and brought them into a politically united country. A hidden political meaning was suspected by the authorities to lie behind several of Verdi's operas, expressing the desire of the Italians for political independence. Even the letters of his name became identified with the initial letters of a political slogan, *Vittorio Emanuele, re d'Italia*, referring to Victor Emanuel, intended king of a united Italy.

Wagner, as we have seen, was ardently in favour of German political unity; and in neighbouring Bohemia Bedřich Smetana and Antonín Dvořák were committed to the cause of their homeland's liberation from the Empire of Austria-Hungary and to the creation of an independent Czech state. Smetana exiled himself for several years as a protest against what he saw as foreign rule from German-speaking Vienna, then returned to Prague to help in the foundation of a Czech national theatre and opera. His most substantial concert work is called, simply, *Má Vlast* ('My Fatherland'), a series of pieces describing the landscape and history of Bohemia. The best-known of these, *Vltava*, follows the course of the river that rises in the Bohemian mountains and flows majestically through Prague. Dvořák, when he was already internationally famous, was invited to spend some time in the United States. There he became interested in the music of the American Negroes

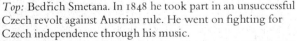

Top: Bedřich Smetana. In 1848 he took part in an unsuccessful Czech revolt against Austrian rule. He went on fighting for Czech independence through his music.
Above: One of the characters from Janáček's opera *The Cunning Little Vixen*, in which he adds the sounds of nature to those of human speech in his music.
Above right: A scene from Finland's national epic poem *The Kalevala*, which Sibelius found a major source of inspiration.

whom he saw, rather like his own Czech people, as a race deprived of their true cultural heritage. Parts of his 'New World' Symphony are based on Negro work songs and spirituals. Dvořák's younger Czech colleague Leoš Janáček believed even more strongly that people everywhere should be proud of their particular culture, including their manner of speech. His own compositions owe much of their very distinctive character to the way they echo the special rhythms and inflections of the Czech language.

All such music can be called nationalistic in one way or another. It expresses the character, hopes and feelings of a particular nation or race of people. In the nineteenth century there was a great deal of nationalism in Europe, and it was by no means confined to those people struggling for political independence. Better education, the

Edvard Grieg. Though he studied at the Leipzig Conservatory, one of the greatest centres of German music, his own compositions are steeped in the songs and dances of his native Norway.

spread of railways and better communications in general made people more informed about the world and more aware of their nation's place in the scheme of things. As a result people of that time developed a stronger sense than their fore-fathers of belonging to one country, of sharing its history and traditions. Composers were aware of this, and many of them wrote music that might stand for their country as clearly as its flag. Besides Smetana and Dvořák there was Manuel de Falla in Spain, Edvard Grieg in Norway and Jean Sibelius in Finland. Each of these composers was the leading musical representative of his country, basing much of his music on national folk songs and dances, or on his nation's history and legends.

In England Edward Elgar was the first great English-born composer since Purcell. Between these two there was a gap of nearly two hundred years, during which most English people thought that the best musicians must be Germans. Handel and his close connection with the German-speaking Hanoverian kings, then Queen Victoria, her German consort Prince Albert, and their special fondness for Mendels-sohn, had largely been responsible for this state of affairs. Elgar, though, proved too great a composer to be ignored by his own countrymen, and he engendered in them a sense of musical pride. He himself was a patriotic artist in the best sense, as were Smetana, Dvořák, Grieg and other musicians elsewhere; a composer who wished to share the spirit and character of his country with people of all nations. He was saddened and dis-mayed that one of his *Pomp and Circumstance* marches became a kind of patriotic hymn during

the First World War with the words 'Land of Hope and Glory'. He hated war and did not want his music associated with fighting and killing. Ralph Vaughan Williams, who was in the army during the war, was one of the next generation of English composers to build upon Elgar's achievements and to create other distinctively English styles of music. Vaughan Williams found his inspiration in English folk song, in the English music of past ages, and in the mystical writings and pictures of John Bunyan and William Blake.

In Russia there was a remarkable group of nationalistic composers known as 'The Five', or 'The Mighty Handful'—Mily Balakirev, César Cui, Alexander Borodin, Modest Mussorgsky,

Nicolai Rimsky-Korsakov. Earlier in the century Mikhail Glinka had emerged as the first Russian composer of any consequence. Before him there was the magnificent tradition of chanting within the Russian Orthodox Church, and a wealth of folk songs and dances, but virtually no composed music of any kind. Russia, vast and impenetrable, had for centuries remained largely isolated from the rest of Europe. With only the example of Glinka as their guide, therefore, 'The Five' had to create a Russian school of music between them. They were all amateurs, to the extent that each, at one time or another, did a completely different job of work. Some were officers of the army or navy. Borodin was a professor of chemistry and never gave up

Facing page: A splendid scene of old Moscow as depicted in Glinka's opera *Ivan Susanin.* Glinka heralded the great age of Russian music in the nineteenth century.
Above: Modest Mussorgsky, painted by Ilya Repin shortly before the composer's death.
Right: Costume design for a boyar, the traditional class of Russian noblemen, as he appears in Mussorgsky's *Boris Godunov.*

this occupation. In a way this general lack of formal musical education helped them, because they found it that much easier to create a strongly individual Russian style. Balakirev, in particular, scorned the academic disciplines of European music and continually urged his colleagues to turn to Asia rather than Europe for their inspiration. Thus many of their compositions evoke the endless horizons of the Russian steppes, or are inspired by colourful and exotic legends of the East. Rimsky-Korsakov based his orchestral suite *Sheherazade* on the *Tales from the Arabian Nights.* This composer had, like Berlioz and Wagner, a superb ear for orchestral 'colour', and it is the vivid, sometimes quite dazzling sound of the orchestration, married to scenes of pure fan-

tasy and adventure, that make *Sheherazade* a favourite with so many people.

Peter Tchaikovsky loved his country as much as 'The Five', and used Russian folk tunes, or melodies based on such folk tunes, in several of his works. 'The people compose, we only write it down,' he once said. In other ways, though, Tchaikovsky's situation was different from that of 'The Five'. He was, apart from a brief period as a civil servant, an academically-trained, fully

This gorgeous stage design by the Russian artist Leon Bakst was for a ballet production of *Sheherazade* set to Rimsky-Korsakov's rich and exotic music.

professional musician who found it comparatively easy to blend his own Russian musical character with the more general style of European music. He was soon one of the most popular composers throughout the Western world. Audiences came to love his broad, sweeping melodies and his dramatic and tempestuous orchestration, as heard in his fantasy overture *Romeo and Juliet*. This composition, which closely follows the events of Shakespeare's play, is very similar to a symphonic poem, and Tchaikovsky's own great gift for descriptive orchestral writing places him with Berlioz and

Liszt as an outstanding composer of Romantic programme music.

A second striking quality of Tchaikovsky's music is its expression of what we think of as the Russian or Slav temperament—moods of deep melancholy set against moments of wild excitement. Nowhere is this side to his music better illustrated than in his Sixth Symphony in B minor, the 'Pathétique'. Writing to a friend about this work, Tchaikovsky said: 'A symphony with a programme, but a programme that will remain an enigma to all. Often while composing it in my mind I shed tears'. Such highly charged emotion, akin to that often conveyed by Mahler, was another feature of much late Romantic music towards the close of the nineteenth century.

As the year 1900 drew near, many musicians of the younger generation were wondering about the future of music. For them the Romantic expression of human thought and feeling that had started with Beethoven and Schubert had gone as far as it could with the music of Tchaikovsky and Mahler. At the same time, the huge Post-Wagnerian orchestra seemed to have become almost an end in itself, with composers like Mahler and Richard Strauss striving to provide it with ever longer, louder and more elaborate scores, burdened with emotion or with heavily-descriptive detail. Thus it was that around the turn of the century several com-

posers, all still comparatively young, turned their backs on what we generally think of as late Romantic or Post-Wagnerian musical styles and set the art of music moving in entirely new directions.

Claude-Achille Debussy in France was one of these. His move away from Romanticism owed something to the fact that the main impetus of Romantic music had come from Germany. During the nineteenth century there had been a succession of distinguished French composers, including Berlioz (actually rather neglected by his own countrymen), Charles Gounod, at one time immensely popular on account of his opera *Faust*, and Georges Bizet whose opera *Carmen* made an even greater impact on the artistic world of his time. Yet it was the German-speaking composers, from Beethoven to Wagner, who dominated the age of Romantic music. It was the

The splendour of nineteenth-century French opera is conveyed in this painting by Edgar Degas. The work being staged is *Robert the Devil* by Meyerbeer whose big spectacular operas were once very popular.

Stage set for the last act of Bizet's *Carmen*, outside the bullring in Seville, where the gipsy heroine is stabbed to death by her lover Don José. The 'Toreador's Song' is a famous aria from this colourful opera.

German army, too, which had triumphed in the Franco-Prussian War of 1870 and humiliated the French. All these things acted on Debussy and helped to shape his creative life. His attitude to Wagner really summed up his position. Like practically everyone else at the end of the nineteenth century, Debussy was spellbound by Wagner's music, but he disliked what he regarded as Wagner's typically German qualities —an intense serious-mindedness and a need to explain and justify everything he did intellectually. 'Old Klingsor' was how Debussy referred to Wagner with a touch of ironic humour, Klingsor being the name of the magician in Wagner's last music drama *Parsifal* who had a terrible hold over other people. It was Debussy's determination to break free from the hold of

Wagner and of German music, together with his own genius, that led him to create one of the most original styles in the whole history of music, and to restore France to the position of a leading musical nation.

One of the most striking features of Debussy's own music is the harmony. As a student he already held strong and independent views on the subject, arguing that a chord has a life and character entirely of its own and need not be related by rule or convention to any other chords or harmonic arrangement of notes. Added to these ideas was his interest in some of the music of antiquity, and his fascination with the oriental music he heard at the time of the Paris Exhibition of 1889 (when the Eiffel Tower was built).

People often compare Debussy's mature musi-

The Deep-Sea Wave off Kanagawa by the Japanese artist Hokusai, one of the sources of inspiration behind Debussy's orchestral masterpiece *La Mer*. Oriental art and music fascinated him.

cal style with the work of Impressionist painters, especially Claude Monet and James McNeill Whistler (whom the composer certainly admired), because he shared with them an interest in such images as rain, mist, water and sunlight. In terms of what he was attempting to do, however, Debussy was probably closer in spirit to a group of French poets, including Stephane Mallarmé and Paul Verlaine, called the Symbolists, who used the evocative power of words and phrases to awaken some image or feeling deep in the reader's mind. Thus we can listen to one of Debussy's greatest orchestral works, *La Mer*, as though it were a marvellous series of pictures of the sea in all its moods; or we can allow the music to strike some answering chord in our own being and so perhaps feel ourselves to

be the very substance and spirit of the waves. His opera, *Pélleas et Mélisande*, is very close in time and place to Wagner's *Tristan und Isolde*, but whereas Wagner's music releases a flood of emotion, Debussy's score perfectly underlines the dream-like atmosphere of a thick forest, where much of the action takes place, and where feelings and passions flare up momentarily and then are lost again.

Debussy wrote much of his finest music for the piano. By the early years of this century the piano had reached its ultimate state of technical refinement, and Debussy drew from it sounds that not even Liszt could have imagined. He distributed notes across the keyboard in an entirely new way, sometimes bunching them together, sometimes placing them at the extreme end of the instrument's compass. He was also at great pains to indicate the use of the sustaining and the soft pedals in order to achieve a special blend of sound, and spoke of the pianist's need always to 'penetrate the notes'. His principal group of piano works are two sets of PRELUDES, using the word as Chopin did to describe pieces which although belonging to a set are complete in themselves. Most of them carry such impressionistic titles as '*Le Vent dans la Plaine*' ('Wind over the Plain'), '*Des Pas sur la Neige*' ('Footprints in the Snow'), '*Feux d'Artifice*' ('Fireworks'); but they convey not so much musical pictures as pure sensation.

Maurice Ravel is often linked with Debussy, as Handel is with Bach, Haydn with Mozart, and Bruckner with Mahler. In each case, the two men concerned did have some musical things in common, while being quite different from each other in outlook and temperament. Ravel wrote some beautiful impressionistic music, and he was a superb orchestrator. The 'Dawn and Sunrise' section from his score to the ballet *Daphnis et Chloé*, depicting the first glimmer of light on the horizon, the awakening of the birds, and the final appearance of the sun flooding the sky with gold, is especially famous. But in other ways, the character of Ravel's music is quite different from that of Debussy. He was, for example, very interested in modelling his own music on past forms and styles. His well-known *Bolero* is modelled on an old Spanish court dance. Likewise, each of his group of piano pieces called *Le Tombeau de Couperin* ('Couperin's Tomb') is written in the form of a French court dance of Couperin's time, though Ravel's own very advanced harmonies belong unmistakably to the twentieth century. Written towards the end of the First World War, each piece is also dedicated to a friend of the composer killed in the fighting, and behind the elegance and polish of the music there can be sensed deep and tender feelings.

Ravel, though an extremely sensitive man, was always careful not to reveal too much personal feeling in his work. In this respect he was completely in step with those other composers, mainly in France, who reacted even more

Another painting by Degas, of ballet dancers. From the age of Louis XIV right up to the time when Diaghilev came to Paris, France was the traditional home of ballet.

strongly than Debussy against what they considered to be the intellectual or emotional heaviness of the Germans. Erik Satie wrote some music to which he gave such names as *Trois Morceaux en forme de poire* ('Three Pear-shaped Pieces'), deliberately intended to shake his audience out of their customary serious state of mind when listening to Beethoven, Brahms or Wagner. Satie and the French writer and artist Jean Cocteau encouraged another group of French composers known as 'Les Six', whose aim was to write music that was light and witty or free from all traditional sentiment. Arthur Honneger, who was actually Swiss by birth, wrote

Les Ballets Russes à Paris

Detail from a programme of Diaghilev's celebrated Russian Ballet. Stravinsky, Debussy, Ravel, Falla and Prokofiev wrote some of their finest music for Diaghilev.

his orchestral piece *Pacific 231* to convey the sound and motion of a railway steam locomotive. It is a notable example of one composer's efforts to come to terms with the unsentimental industrial and mechanical world of the twentieth century, and makes an interesting comparison with a film of the same period, Charlie Chaplin's *Modern Times*, which is also to do with the relationship between man and machinery.

Igor Stravinsky, another major figure in the development of twentieth-century music, put the attitude of 'Les Six' and most of his contemporaries in a nutshell when he said of heavily emotional Romantic music, 'the crowd expects the composer to tear out his entrails and exhibit them!'. Stravinsky, Russian by birth but later a French and then an American citizen, made a tremendous impact on the musical world with the scores he composed for the Diaghilev Ballet. France was the traditional home of ballet, dating back to the time of Louis XIV and the opera-ballets at the court of Versailles. Russia, which developed strong cultural links with France dur-

ing the eighteenth and nineteenth centuries, then became famous for the ballet music of its composers, notably Tchaikovsky, and for its own ballet companies. Sergei Diaghilev established his ballet company in France, and during the early years of this century commissioned music, stage and costume designs from many of the most gifted composers and artists of the time, as well as employing the greatest dancers and choreographers. Among the latter was Vaslav Nijinsky. For a long time prior to him most of the greatest dancers had been the female ballerinas. However, with his artistry and technique, including his phenomenal leaps high into the air, Nijinsky helped restore the importance of male ballet dancing and indeed became one of the most celebrated dancers of all time.

Stravinsky's three scores for Diaghilev's Russian Ballet showed him advancing by creative leaps and bounds from someone still obviously influenced by his studies with Rimsky-Korsakov to a composer of outstanding originality and daring. The first was *L'Oiseau de feu*

('The Firebird'), based on an old Russian fairy story about a fabulous bird of fire. Next came *Petrushka*, the portrayal of a puppet and of his tragic life of love and jealousy behind the scenes of a travelling theatre, set against the colourful background of the Shrove Tide Fair in old St Petersburg. Third was *Le Sacre du printemps* ('The Rite of Spring'), which depicted the savage rituals of a pagan Russia. This could certainly be called emotional music, but not of the kind that Stravinsky so scorned. One of the composer's most original strokes of genius was to open his score with a solo bassoon playing in its highest register. Nothing could better set the scene of a huge and desolate landscape slowly awakening to a bleak, cold light. It was, however, the music that followed, culminating in a wild sacrificial dance to the forces of nature, that caused the famous uproar at the first performance in Paris in 1913. The work has long been a twentieth-century classic, familiar to all music lovers, but

at the time of that first performance music of such complexity and of such violence had never been heard before, and the audience must have thought the world really was coming to an end.

Two other composers who broke decisively with all established convention and played an important part in shaping the music of our century were Béla Bartók and Arnold Schoenberg. The folk music of his native Hungary and of neighbouring Romania were Bartók's starting point. The nationalist composers before Bartók had usually taken what they wanted from the folk music of their respective countries and dressed it up in their own musical style. Liszt's Hungarian Rhapsodies and Dvořák's Slavonic Dances are two examples of this. Such a process did not satisfy Bartók. For him folk music was not something to be taken out of its true context and beautified. Its real character must be preserved. So he travelled across the broad plains of Hungary and up into the remote mountain re-

Costume designs for Stravinsky's ballet *Pulcinella*. Based on the music of Pergolesi and other eighteenth-century composers, it is one of Stravinsky's so-called 'Neo-Classical' works (see also page 163).

Polish folk dancers. Nineteenth-century nationalist composers used folk songs and dances to give their music 'local colour'. Bartók re-created such melodies and rhythms in an exciting new way.

gions of Transylvania (home of the vampire legends!) taking note of every folk song and dance that he heard. In this way he absorbed folk melodies and rhythms so thoroughly that he did not need to copy and adapt them to fit into his own music, as others had done. They became the very life-blood of his composition: tough, earthy, elemental, and strongly coloured by the intervals and harmonies of other folk music from further east. Bartók was a shy, gentle person who opened up exciting new prospects for the use of melody and rhythm in music, and also brought a

new kind of beauty to his art. But many of the people who first heard his compositions probably imagined him, as they imagined Stravinsky, to be a strange and wild sort of man.

Arnold Schoenberg started writing music that was heavily Post-Wagnerian in style. His *Gurrelieder* ('Songs of Gurra'), for example, is written for soloists, several choruses and an enormous orchestra which includes such special sound effects as iron chains to evoke a gloomy medieval castle. Schoenberg then started to react against such a style of composition, but in a

Above: Portrait of Arnold Schoenberg by the Russian artist Oscar Kokoschka. Schoenberg himself was a talented artist and painted the portrait of Alban Berg (*above left*), one of his chief musical disciples.

manner quite different from that of Debussy, Stravinsky or Bartók. While they evolved out of their work new kinds of musical language, Schoenberg conceived a new musical 'grammar' on which his work might be based. The most important part of this was his idea of a 'tone-row' to replace the established system of twenty-four major and minor keys. A tone-row was to

consist of all twelve notes, as they exist on the black and white keys of a piano between any octave, placed in a particular order, or series. The significant thing about a tone-row was that all twelve notes were of equal tonal value, as distinct from a major or minor scale, in which each note has a special relationship with the rest. Schoenberg's tone-rows really were like a new musical

Three characters from Kodály's *Háry János* (see also page 144). In this opera, and the orchestral suite drawn from it, Kodály includes the cimbalom (*above*), a stringed instrument widely used in Hungarian folk music.

alphabet, and when he started writing what was called TWELVE-TONE (or DODECAPHONIC) music based on them, people were at first completely baffled and perplexed.

Schoenberg also created a method of singing called *Sprechgesang* ('speech-song'), by which the singer glides between the pitch of a sequence of notes rather than holding the pitch of each note as he or she would in a normal song. He developed this technique to the full in his song-cycle *Pierrot Lunaire* ('Moonstruck Pierrot'). In the poems that Schoenberg here set to music, the traditional pantomime figure of Pierrot is taken to symbolize the sad, broken spirit of modern man. To the basic pessimism of these poems,

Schoenberg's music adds a dream-like and sometimes quite nightmarish quality. He composed it at the time when Sigmund Freud and other pioneer psychiatrists were first beginning to delve deeply into the inner workings of the mind. An interesting parallel can be drawn between their scientific investigations of the human mind and artistic interest in the subject as shown by Schoenberg, by the 'stream of consciousness' writing of authors such as James Joyce, and by the surrealist paintings of Salvador Dali, Max Ernst and others. In fact, Schoenberg himself had studied painting with one of the leading artists of the Expressionist school, Kandinsky.

While Schoenberg was reshaping European music with much thought and effort, a musical revolution of a very different kind was taking place in America. The United States, a nation since 1776, had grown in area, population and economic power faster than any other nation in history. It had also produced, in men like George Washington and Abraham Lincoln, Edgar Allen Poe, Henry Wadsworth Longfellow and Mark Twain, some of the greatest political leaders and writers of their age. In music, however, it had not shone so brightly. German musicians ran many of its musical institutions (as they did in England during the same period), and most American composers wrote music that sounded as though it copied the work of Chopin, Schumann or Liszt. Dvořák was among the first to say that American composers should try to speak with a stronger musical voice of their own. 'America can have her own music, a fine music growing up from her own soil and having its own special character,' he declared soon after his arrival in the United States. He was referring to the spirituals and work songs of the American Negroes. What he could not foresee was that within a few years of his death this music would blaze forth with a vitality and power that was largely its own and did not need any 'serious' composer to help it develop.

This was JAZZ. Its origins are bound up with the shameful story of how millions of Africans were sold into slavery and shipped across the Atlantic for work in the Americas, especially on the cotton plantations of Georgia, Louisiana, Mississippi and other southern states of the United States. One of the strongest features of their music was rhythm. This was something much more potent than a white man's idea of straightforward beats to the bar. The American Negroes' sense of rhythm was inherited from their African ancestors, whose tribal drums conveyed their strongest and deepest feelings, so that when they danced it was with their souls as well as their bodies. Another striking feature of this Negro music was improvization. As with all folk music, their songs were not 'composed' in the

The New Orleans waterfront in 1884, with its bales of cotton and Mississippi river boats. The city attracted thousands of black people from the old plantations. A few years later it became the birthplace of jazz.

usual European sense of that word. No one person wrote them. They were common property, growing and changing all the time, as each person and each generation came to them. They were improvized upon—recreated—with every rendering.

The events which changed the lives of the American Negroes and brought about the true beginnings of jazz were the American Civil War of 1861 to 1865 and President Lincoln's abolition of slavery. The war itself had ruined most of the cotton plantations, and thousands of officially 'free' but jobless Negroes drifted into the towns and cities of the South, and especially into the port of New Orleans. 'The Crescent City' as it was called, because of the way it had spread round a wide curve of the Mississippi river, had been founded by French explorers and traders, then became a Spanish possession, before finally joining the United States early in the nineteenth century. It also had a large Creole population—people of mixed Negro, French, Spanish and Portuguese descent. The new arrivals found it relatively easy to mix with the Creole people, and soon learnt some of their songs and dances, many of which were of French or Spanish

When Henri Toulouse-Lautrec painted this picture in Paris jazz was just beginning to take shape in America's Deep South. The black dancer (*Chocolat dansant*) vividly portrayed here symbolizes the rhythms and vitality of jazz and the influence it was soon to have on European music.

New Orleans funeral parade. When the mourners broke into a spontaneous kind of dance they were honouring the dead, not insulting them, with their instinctive sense of rhythm.

origin. They also found it quite easy to acquire musical instruments, left behind by the old Confederate army bands at the end of the Civil War. Such were the circumstances that assisted in the birth of jazz. Nobody is quite sure how the word 'jazz' actually came into being. One theory is that it came from the French word *jaser*, meaning 'to gossip' or 'chat', as used to describe the way early jazz musicians improvised, or chatted together on their instruments. At all events, by the beginning of this century those who played it, or sang and danced to it, knew quite clearly what they meant by jazz.

Much of their music was brash and spirited. Rival bands meeting at street corners would often stand and play against each other until one band had literally blown itself out with exhaustion. There were frequent street parades organized by groups or societies with such colourful names as Hobgoblins and Original Swells. Jazz bands were also in attendance at funerals, leading the mourners in a kind of shuffling dance. 'Rags' and 'stomps' were the names given to this kind of music. But there was also BLUES, the most enduring and influential of all jazz forms. People had used the word 'blue' to describe a mood of sadness or melancholy long before the American Negroes, but it was their Blues that have given the word its real significance in this context. All the old classic Blues numbers were a kind of lament. They were often rendered in their original form by a singer who inserted the basic Blues harmonies between each phrase with a few chords on a mouth organ. Such music-making was very simple and rough by European standards, but a good Blues singer could express himself with a directness and force that no white man could match. Hunger, loneliness, destitution are the recurring themes of the Blues. 'I can't make a nickel, I'm flat as can be; Some people say money is talking, but it won't say a word to me,' are the words of the 'Hard Time Blues'.

By the end of the First World War musicians such as Joe 'King' Oliver, Edward 'Kid' Ory, Ferdinand 'Jelly Roll' Morton and Louis Armstrong had set jazz firmly on its path, and their music was spreading, by way of the Mississippi river, to other cities like St Louis and Chicago. It was also changing. New Orleans, with its old-world charm and sub-tropical climate, had kept

Above: Colourful impression of a Mississippi show boat. The kind of minstrel shows associated with these boats became popular in America and Europe, though real jazz men scorned such music.

Left: Hard Times is the title of this very atmospheric painting of a traditional Blues singer.

A picture that captures very well the bright, brash spirit of jazz
at about the time of the First World War.

Miles Davis (born 1926) developed one of the most distinctive trumpet sounds in jazz and did much to create the new 'cool', rather spare jazz style of the 1950s.

jazz sounding fresh and rather innocent. Chicago, an industrial city of the north, with its smoke and tenements, gave to the music a tough, hard edge. The old Blues, for example, were speeded up into a machine-like piano style called BOOGIE WOOGIE, originally the name of a dance. Charlie 'Cow Cow' Davenport was a pioneer of boogie. He took his nickname from the iron cowcatcher on the front of the giant steam locomotives that thundered across the continent bringing grain and meat to Chicago. Another famous boogie pianist was Clarence 'Pine Top' Smith, killed in a dance hall shoot-out. This was the Prohibition period, when gangsters like Al Capone virtually ran Chicago and other cities through their control of the illicit liquor trade.

It was this sort of thing that had so far given jazz a bad reputation among white Americans and Europeans. Although the new fashionable dances that came in during and just after the First World War, like the CHARLESTON, had a snappy,

jazz-like quality, they were still comfortably removed from the real thing with its rather sordid associations. What finally brought jazz a wider audience and greatly improved its public image was the arrival on the scene of men like Edward 'Duke' Ellington and William 'Count' Basie. They recruited to their bands musicians with academic training and made special arrangements, or even composed original pieces, for them to play. There were some people then, as there are still some today, who argue that writing jazz down and playing it from the written music kills its true spirit. Many more people, though, were impressed by this new professional style of jazz, and intrigued by the way it either smoothed out or tightened up the basic jazz rhythms into a special kind of SYNCOPATION. Handel, Haydn, Mozart, Beethoven and many other European composers of the past had used syncopation—the shifting of the beat in a passage of music to give it extra emphasis

85

Earl 'Fatha' Hines (born 1905), veteran jazz pianist and band leader.

or momentum—but Ellington, Basie and their colleagues combined their sophisticated new style of playing with the black man's inborn sense of rhythm. From first bar to last, their music was borne along by syncopation. This marked the beginning of SWING, and the entry of jazz into the main stream of white American and European popular music.

For many people jazz and dance music then came to mean virtually the same thing, although serious jazz musicians continued to develop their art along lines which carried it far from its simple origins. Charlie Parker and Dizzy Gillespie, for example, created the style known as BEBOP, which broke away from all the established ideas about jazz melody and rhythm and was as revolutionary in its way as the music of Bartók or Schoenberg.

The origins of jazz, its growth, and the way its rhythms and harmonies, its special kinds of melody and its use of instruments, flowed into the broader currents of Western dance and popular music, happened to coincide almost exactly with the invention and development of sound recording. The principle of acoustic recording, by which sound vibrations could be registered as grooves of varying depth or direction upon certain surfaces (originally tin foil), then picked up

Two of the greatest names in jazz. *Above:* Louis Armstrong, affectionately called 'Satchmo'. *Above right:* 'Duke' Ellington leading his band from the piano. Both men kept the same high standards for nearly fifty years.
Right: A classic jazz recording on an old 78r.p.m. disc, now a collector's item.

again and reproduced as sound, had first been demonstrated by the American Thomas Alva Edison in 1877. In the years that followed, some very distinguished people were persuaded to record a few brief words, or a brief passage of music, including Gladstone, Tennyson and Bismarck, Hans von Bülow, famous pianist and conductor, and Brahms. No doubt they were all astonished, in the excitement of the moment, to hear themselves played back at the turn of a

The jive and jitterbug matched the rhythmic punch of boogie and the best of swing. After them came rock n' roll.

handle (von Bülow is said to have fainted), but these were little more than novelty experiments, for the voices or music were mostly so faint and distorted as to be virtually unrecognizable.

The first recordings of good quality used discs instead of Edison's original cylinder-designed phonograph, together with a new way of registering the sound vibrations, and a much improved method of transferring the recording from a master to a large number of duplicate discs. They were made during the early years of this century by some of the great operatic stars of the time, notably Enrico Caruso and Dame Nellie Melba. However, the first records that many people bought for their own enjoyment were of the Charleston and other jazz-inspired dances that swept across America and Europe at the time of the First World War. Some of the great founder-figures of jazz, including 'Jelly Roll' Morton and Louis Armstrong, also made records at about the same time. Then, during the 1920s, as jazz was spreading upwards and outwards like a tree from its roots in New Orleans, so the old acoustic method of recording was replaced by electrical recording. No longer did musicians and singers have to crowd round a large acoustic horn so that their performance could be transferred directly to a recording disc. Instead, microphones picked up their music, and it was recorded electronically with a strength and clarity impossible to achieve before. The recording of symphonies, operas and other kinds of 'serious' music benefited enormously from these technical advances; but it was a specially happy event for the new big jazz and swing bands that electrical recording and new mass production methods came in when they did, to make their kind of music readily available to people all over the world.

The most notable feature of the big swing

Humorous painting of the tango, one of the Latin American dances that were all the rage in the 1920s. Ravel, Stravinsky and Walton were three composers who parodied the popular dances of this time.

bands that went on to dominate popular music in America and Europe during the 1930s and 1940s was their prominent use of saxophones. The saxophone, a cross between a brass and a woodwind instrument, had been invented in the nineteenth century. Bizet and a few other composers made occasional use of it, but it did not really come into its own until the jazz and dance band era. It became the chosen instrument of some of the most gifted and original of jazzmen. Above all, it was the large saxophone sections maintained by such famous band leaders of the swing period as Artie Shaw and Glenn Miller—the instruments being graded in size and pitch in a way very similar to a Renaissance consort of viols or recorders—that became such a familiar sound to millions through the medium of radio and the gramophone record.

After the Second World War, the existing type of gramophone record disc, with its 78 revolutions per minute and limited playing time, was replaced by the Long Playing record; and swing was replaced by ROCK N' ROLL. In its original form, rock n' roll was quite like a vocalized form of boogie, and so carried forward something of the spirit of jazz right through the 1950s and into the 1960s. At the same time, Elvis Presley and other stars of rock n' roll brought about another instrumental revolution, by transforming the guitar from a rather solitary and aristocratic type of instrument, associated mainly with Spanish FLAMENCO singing, into the glossy, streamlined and electronically amplified symbol of the strident world of pop music. After him it was The Beatles who, during the early 1960s, rose swiftly to the top of this commercial empire of sound. Coming from Liverpool, they were practically the first Europeans to influence styles in popular music on a world-wide scale since jazz had given America the lead earlier in the twentieth century.

Many of the greatest composers of this century have been influenced by jazz. Before the First World War Debussy was already writing pieces like the 'Golliwog's Cakewalk' (from his *Children's Corner* suite for piano), based on an early jazz dance rhythm. Ravel, who was still composing right through the 1920s, took a deeper interest in jazz, and his Violin Sonata has a movement actually called 'Blues'. Stravinsky too wrote some clever parodies of early jazz styles, and later composed his 'Ebony' Concerto for the jazz clarinettist Woody Herman. There

The glamour of Broadway, centre of American show business, against a background of Manhattan skyscrapers—the perfect setting for Gershwin's *Rhapsody in Blue*.

was also Kurt Weill, who was working in Berlin during the 1920s. Berlin was at that time much troubled by political agitation and violence due to Germany's defeat in the First World War and the terrible inflation that followed. It was at the same time a lively centre of the arts, which encouraged Weill and the dramatist Bertold Brecht to write several unusual operas in which they exposed the corruption and squalor of their rather feverish society. To achieve the sharp and sardonic musical effect he wanted, Weill drew upon the basic instrumentation and playing styles of early jazz. 'Mack the Knife' from the opera *Die Dreigroschenoper* ('The Threepenny Opera') is the best-known song that Weill and Brecht wrote together. It is interesting to note that many years later Louis Armstrong, one of the founder-figures of jazz, took this song back and made it one of his greatest hits and a tune instantly recognized by thousands of his fans who are unaware of its true origin and composers and who know nothing about 'The Threepenny Opera'.

In America itself composers were quick to recognize jazz as their country's most original contribution to the world of music. Aaron Copland, who has often used his music to portray different aspects of American life and history, brought jazz rhythms into several of his compositions. But no one is more closely identified with jazz in the concert hall than George Gershwin. With his brother Ira, who wrote many of his lyrics, George Gershwin was already one of America's leading song writers when the band leader Paul Whiteman asked him to write a 'symphonic' piece of jazz. The result was the *Rhapsody in Blue*, originally written for piano and a large jazz or dance band, but now more usually arranged for a full orchestra. It is like a musical kaleidoscope, mixing and blending points of style from the Romantic concertos of Tchaikovsky and Rachmaninov with a rapid succession of jazz and sometimes Latin American rhythms, harmonies and instrumental effects. There is also one fine big tune that Tchaikovsky, had he lived on Manhattan Island instead of Moscow, could have been proud of. Gershwin,

who pursued his career as a serious composer, took lessons in orchestration and composition and went on to write the all-Negro opera *Porgy and Bess* containing some of his most beautiful songs; but his *Rhapsody in Blue* is still the piece that many people love best.

Gershwin succeeded in reaching a wide audience because his music was relatively uncomplicated and written as genuine entertainment. Other twentieth-century composers, perhaps with deeper musical knowledge than Gershwin, have also tried to give audiences music they can understand and enjoy, while being true to their own creative selves. In the Soviet Union the duty of the artist to serve the community in one way or another has long been official Marxist policy, and major composers like Sergei Prokofiev and Dmitri Shostakovich have done their best to conform to this. Prokofiev left the Soviet Union as a young man and composed some very advanced music for his time, but when he returned home he modified his style in accord with government wishes, writing such pieces as *Peter and the Wolf*, the ballet music to *Romeo and Juliet*, and many film scores, which have indeed been enjoyed by millions, inside and outside the Soviet Union. Shostakovich's fifteen symphonies, forming the central part of his output, are mostly big, musically quite straightforward but serious-minded works. Their intention has been not so much to entertain as to inspire audiences, with their frequent reference to revolutionary or heroic episodes in Soviet history.

Outside the Soviet Union, where composers have been free from political control, some have still tried to serve the community through their work. Copland, Leonard Bernstein and Gian-Carlo Menotti in the United States have each written music intended to entertain or to express religious or moral ideas in styles that most people can understand. In Germany Paul Hindemith composed a great deal of what is called *Gebrauchsmusik*, a term translated rather unhappily as 'Utility Music', but meaning music intended for people to learn and play together and so serving a useful social purpose. In England Benjamin Britten shared with his older colleague Vaughan

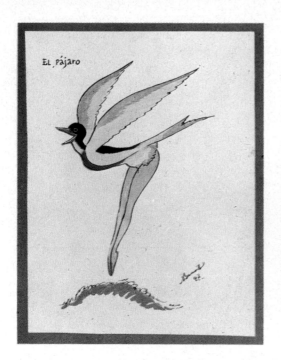

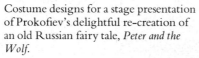

Costume designs for a stage presentation of Prokofiev's delightful re-creation of an old Russian fairy tale, *Peter and the Wolf*.

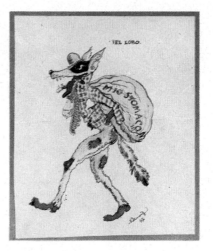

Williams the desire to relate his work to the great heritage of English literature and folk music and so create a recognizable link between the past and the present. Britten made many arrangements of traditional folk songs and set to music poems taken from various periods of English history. In *Peter Grimes*, based on a story of the Suffolk coast where Britten himself lived for much of his life, he also wrote one of the few operas this century to become a standard work in the opera repertory. At the same time, Britten was interested in the art and music of many parts of the world, his

short opera *Curlew River* (also described as 'A Parable for Church Performance') being based on a medieval Japanese play.

Composers such as Hindemith, Shostakovich and Britten could be called musical conservatives because they produced most of their work in well-established forms and did not advance too far ahead of their listeners. Other composers of our time have been called *avant-garde* (a French term generally taken to mean 'ahead of their time'), because they have wished to explore and develop new possibilities in music. They have often done this in the face of almost complete public indifference—a growing problem for many artists since Beethoven—but their work is of great value and relevance to the age we live in.

One of the main concerns of so-called *avant-garde* composers has been with the creation of new kinds of musical sound. Sometimes they have used what most people would consider quite unmusical sounds, such as car horns, police sirens and whistles, not just for the sake of novelty but to relate their music more closely to the urban, industrialized society most of us belong to. The Italian composer Luigi Nono, in his composition *La Fabbrica Illuminata*, uses recordings made in a metal works to convey factory conditions. Another way in which musicians of our age have extended the boundaries of musical sound has been to use conventional instruments in unconventional ways. John Cage in America attracted considerable interest with his 'prepared piano'. Cage 'prepared' his piano by placing objects over or between the strings so as radically to alter its usual playing qualities. He could also strike the keys in certain ways, in conjunction with the pedals, or pluck the strings, in order to produce other unusual effects.

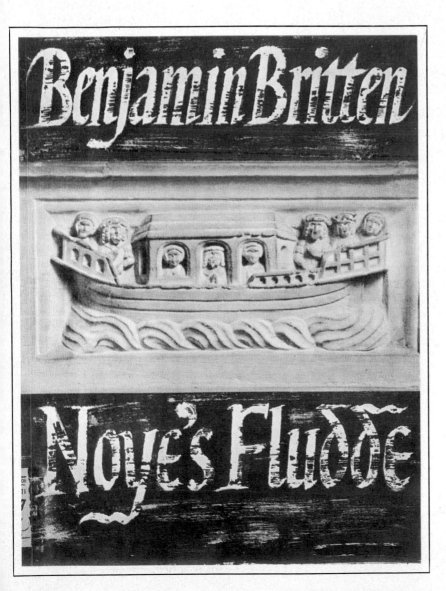

Cover to an edition of Britten's stage work *Noye's Fludde*, one of several he wrote specially for church performance. The spelling of the title is old English for 'Noah's Flood', and Britten based the work on a medieval Miracle Play. Stravinsky's musical play *The Flood* has the same historical source.

Setting for a scene from Berg's very moving opera *Wozzeck*, which makes use of Schoenberg's vocal style of *Sprechgesang* or 'speech-song' (see also page 79).

Cage has been a leading figure among those who have wanted people to listen to sounds in new and unprejudiced ways. His piece called *Imaginary Landscapes* uses a group of radio sets, which he instructs to be raised and lowered in volume in a particular sequence, the object being to get his audience to listen closely to what they might ordinarily dismiss as random and unimportant sounds. Another point about *Imaginary Landscapes* is that no two hearings of it can be the same, because the radio sets will always be receiving different broadcasts. The word used to describe such a situation is ALEATORY. This comes from the Latin *alea*, meaning 'dice', and like the throw of the dice, there is always an element of chance in aleatory music. Similar to this is the idea of 'indeterminacy' which modern composers sometimes use. Here they plan their music so that performers are given a number of options as to when and at what point in the score they start to play, or finish playing.

Most significant during the second half of this century has been the development of electronic music. Conventional instruments that were electrically amplified, or instruments with some electronic source of sound, started to be made before the First World War, and during the 1920s and 1930s an interesting range of these was available to musicians. Olivier Messiaen, a composer whose musical thinking has given us many fascinating and beautiful sounds, has made use of one of these electronic instruments called the *Ondes Martenot*. The pure, rather unearthly sound of the instrument can be heard to remarkable effect in this composer's 'Turangalîla' Symphony, where it soars above orchestral passages of great rhythmic and harmonic complexity. These, and the symphony's very unusual title, are all a part of Messiaen's deep interest in Indian music and mysticism.

It was, however, the invention of the tape recorder during the Second World War that really opened the gates to a whole new universe of sound. Musicians were quick to realize that with two tape recorders they could record and re-record sounds almost indefinitely, constantly changing the quality and character of the sounds by playing them back at different speeds or in reverse, or by cutting up the tape and reassembling the sections in a new order. One early cen-

Stage set for Hindemith's opera *Mathis der Maler*, about the
German Renaissance painter Matthias Grünewald.

tre for such experiments was the studios of the
French Broadcasting Company in Paris. It was
here that the term *musique concrète* was applied.
Everyday, or 'concrete', sounds were recorded
and then dissected and reassembled on tapes according to principles quite similar to those used
by some artists who take everyday objects and
reassemble them as an abstract or semi-abstract
collage. Pierre Boulez, a pupil of Messiaen and
one of today's most penetrating musical
thinkers, was an early exponent of *musique concrète*. Since then multi-track recorders, synthesizers (which can analyse and reproduce every
imaginable quality of sound) and quadrophonic
sound reproduction has made the musician's
studio seem more like a space-age laboratory.

Karlheinz Stockhausen has made wonderfully
imaginative use of electronic sound in a number
of his works. He also shares, with Messiaen and
others, a deep sense of the timeless, mystical
qualities of music, which refers back to the dis-
tant past as well as to the future. In his composition *Stimmung* ('Tuning') he returns to that most
basic and natural instrument of all, the human
voice. The work is based on one chord, made up
rather like the notes in a harmonic series. Six
vocalists continually repeat this chord into microphones, so that the balance of the voices can be
adjusted electronically, first one note and then
another of the harmony standing out from the
rest. At the same time the singers recite a list of
'magic words' taken from many religions, in the
manner of a mantra—the private call to medi-
tation. As Stockhausen has said of this extraordinary piece of music:

'Certainly *Stimmung* is meditative music.

Above: Stage design for Bartók's *The Miraculous Mandarin*. This ballet and the same composer's one-act opera *Duke Bluebeard's Castle* carry a deeper psychological meaning behind the actual stage events.
Left: Scriabin's design for an edition of his symphonic poem *Prometheus, Poem of Fire* (see also page 159). This composer's interest in mysticism has been taken up by many later twentieth-century musicians.

Time is suspended. One listens to the inner self of the sound, the inner self of the harmonic spectrum, the inner self of the vowel, *the inner self*. Subtlest fluctuations, scarcely a ripple, *all the senses* alert and calm. In the beauty of the sensual shines the beauty of the eternal.'

For centuries Western music was firmly based on the idea that a composition, however simple, must have a recognizable form and progress from one definite point to another. In this century men like Stockhausen and some of the best jazz, rock and pop musicians have revealed to us another side of the wonderful experience we call music.

Musical Instruments

Sounds are combinations of pitch, volume and tone. When they are indiscriminately mixed together we call them noise. When they are acoustically fashioned and balanced we consider them as musical sounds. The musical instruments which men and women have devised to produce the desired blends of pitch, volume and tone have themselves been combinations of a few basic factors—namely, the source of sound, materials, size and shape. We may liken the factors that go to make up musical instruments, and the factors that go to make up sounds, to the two sides of an equation. Take away or add something to the structure of an instrument and we bring about a corresponding change in the nature and quality of the sound. This is the fascinating story of musical instruments and the way they are played.

Their scientific classification, using terms of Greek origin, is according to their source of sound:

Idiophones are instruments of wood or metal that vibrate within themselves when struck. Wood blocks as used in varying sizes in a xylophone, cymbals, gongs and bells are all idiophones.

Membranophones are instruments that use a stretched membrane, hide or skin as their basic source of sound. Drums are the principal types of membranophone.

Aerophones are instruments requiring a column of air to be set in motion inside a tube or pipe, usually by the player's own breath. Whistles, flutes, recorders, horns, trumpets, organs are all aerophones.

Chordophones are instruments whose source of sound is the vibration of a tightly drawn string or wire. The violin and cello, harp and guitar, piano and harpsichord are examples of chordophones. The human voice might also be considered as a chordophone, although it also needs our own breath to make it sound.

There is, however, an alternative system of classification, which divides the majority of instruments up into percussion, strings, woodwind and brass. It places such instruments as the piano and organ into the special category of keyboard instruments. This is the classification best known to music-lovers, and the one we shall follow here.

Percussion Instruments

These are instruments that are struck in some manner—drums, gongs, cymbals, bells and more local and specialized instruments such as castanets. Within this broad family of percussion instruments, the big division is between those of definite and those of indefinite pitch.

Many drums are percussion instruments of definite pitch. They have a membranous playing-surface tightly stretched over a bowl-shaped frame which acts as a resonator—i.e. it amplifies and to a certain extent modifies the sound of the vibrating membrane. Traditionally

97

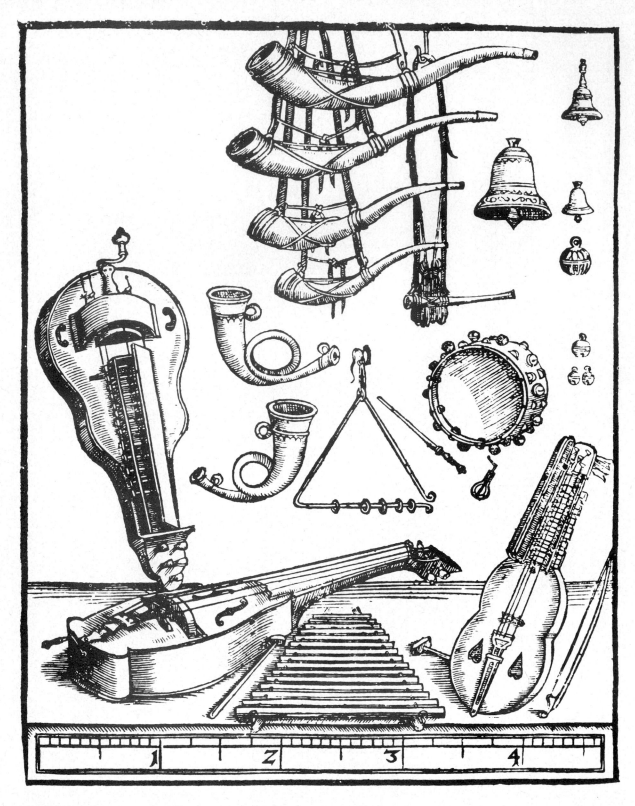

This fine old German print includes instruments belonging to
each of the four scientifically defined groups.

Opening of Beethoven's *Eroica* symphony showing how the instruments in a score are organized into woodwind, brass percussion and strings.

Traditional type of kettledrum from South India.

this membrane was made of animal hide, which in the past often included human skin; and it was a common belief that to play such a drum was to call up the spirit of the dead animal or person. The matter of pitch is determined both by the size of the drum and by the tightness of the membrane. A drum with a large playing-surface and correspondingly large resonator will produce a much deeper-pitched note than one constructed on a smaller scale. At the same time, a very tightly stretched membrane will vibrate quicker and so produce a higher-pitched note than a membrane that is comparatively slack.

In an orchestra the principal percussion instruments of definite pitch are the kettledrums, or timpani. They can be tuned by adjusting the tightness of the membrane. At one time this was done by screws placed round the rim of the playing-surface. Today kettledrums are tuned by the operation of a pedal, which is not only more efficient but allows the player to strike his drum and then quickly adjust the tension in the membrane so as to produce a note that glides up or down in pitch. Composers have long used kettledrums not so much to keep a steady beat going as to point up certain chords and to add weight to the body of orchestral sound. Their orchestral role is therefore mainly a supporting one, although composers have occasionally given them small solo parts. Haydn's 'Drumroll' Symphony owes its nickname to the fact that it opens with a roll on the kettledrum. Beethoven opens his Violin Concerto with four notes on the kettledrums, and also makes dramatic use of them in the great scherzo of his Ninth Symphony. Gershwin brings in towards the end of his Piano Concerto in F a solo passage for

Starting young on the triangle, cymbals, tubular bells and drums (plus guitar and recorder).

kettledrums which clearly demonstrates their quality of definite pitch.

The xylophone is obviously a percussion instrument of definite pitch, its individual wooden blocks graded in size to produce a scale. The glockenspiel (German for 'bell-play'), which has metal bars; the marimba, a traditional type of Latin American xylophone; and the vibraphone, in which the sounds are sustained and modified by a special set of electrically-operated resonators (very popular in some jazz and dance music), are all based on the same principle.

The other important group of percussion instruments of definite pitch are bells. Nothing could demonstrate better the direct relationship between pitch, tone and volume of sound on the one hand, and instrumental size and shape on the other, than the contrast between the delicate tinkle of a small hand-bell and the massive, sonorous tolling of a bell weighing several tons.

Percussion instruments of indefinite pitch are more numerous. They include other types of drum—side drums (of which the medieval tabor is an early example) and the similarly constructed but larger bass drums; gongs and cymbals; the tambourine, triangle and castanets. In the orchestra it is the percussion section that also accommodates any other special-effect instruments composers sometimes ask for, even when they are not technically percussion instruments at all—from whips and rattles to car horns and wind machine (a device consisting of a broad strip of canvas stretched tightly over two large revolving cylinders or drums).

Stringed Instruments

The big division among stringed instruments is between those designed to be plucked and those whose strings are primarily intended to be set in motion by a bow.

The most ancient and widespread type of plucked stringed instrument is the harp. Fundamentally the harp consists of a set of strings stretched across a frame, each of different length (and perhaps of different thickness also), so producing notes of different pitch. The frame must also act as a resonator, giving volume and tone to the basic sound of the strings. There are many drawings or paintings of harps on the walls of Egyptian palaces or tombs, dating back thousands of years. A few actual specimens of these have survived. Other ancient versions of the harp are the lyre, much favoured by the Greeks, Assyrians and Hebrews, and the two main types of pre-Christian Celtic harp, the Welsh telyn and Irish clàrsach. A truly remarkable instrument was the Aeolian harp: here the strings were set in motion not by any human agent but by the action of the wind (the instrument being named after Aeolus, legendary Greek keeper of the winds). The effect is similar to that sometimes heard when the wind blows across telegraph wires, and to the Greeks, with their mystical beliefs, it was interpreted as the divine voice of the wind and of nature.

Ancient Egyptian (and one Persian) harps, illustrated in a nineteenth-century volume.

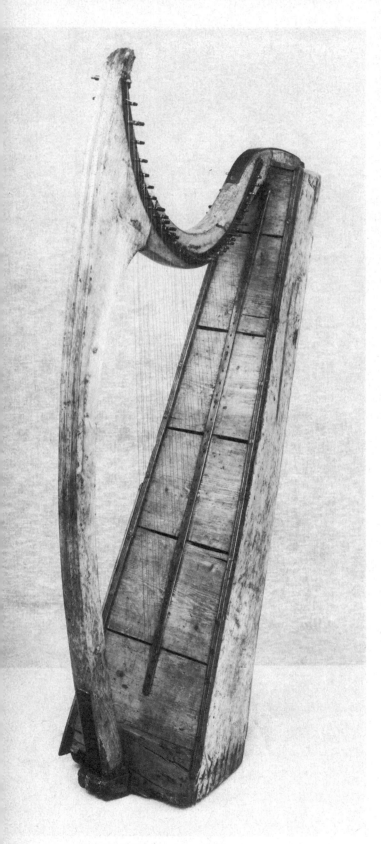

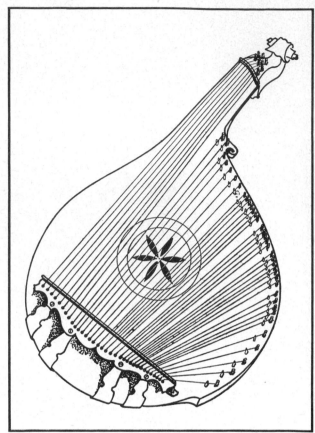

Left: A beautiful example of a traditional Irish harp.
Above: The bandoura, a traditional Russian stringed instrument.
Facing page: Pedal harp made in 1858 by the Paris firm of Erard. This famous company also made pianos.

The modern type of harp, dating from the early nineteenth century, is a large instrument with pedals which can adjust the pitch of the strings and allow the harpist a wide range of notes. It also made its way into the orchestra during the last century, adding glitter and richness to orchestral sound. Few composers have written for it as a solo instrument—Ravel's Introduction and Allegro for Flute, Harp and String Quartet being an exception—although Harpo Marx showed how attractive it could sound entirely on its own in the famous Marx Brothers films.

Above: Two eighteenth-century English citterns. These instruments are sometimes called 'English guitars'.
Left: Three characters dressed for a Renaissance play or masque. The one on the left is tuning a lute.

Other plucked stringed instruments are designed on the more familiar pattern of a neck attached to a resonating body, the strings being stretched down the length of the instrument. Such instruments do not have a separate string for each note. Instead, the player adjusts the effective playing length of a limited number of strings by pressing them against the neck at selected points with the fingers of one hand, a process called stopping. By Renaissance times there were plucked stringed instruments of a wide range called citterns and theorbos. Above all there was the lute, which inspired some of the finest instrumental music of the period. Today, the best-known plucked stringed instrument is the guitar, whose direct ancestor was the Spanish vihuela. Others are the mandolin (similar to a

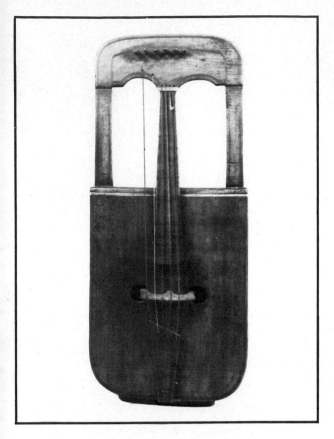

Above: The Celtic crwth, one of the earliest types of stringed instruments played with a bow.
Right: Handsome cello (violincello), dated 1711, made by the School of Stradivarius.

lute), the banjo, the ukelele and the Russian balalaika.

A very early example of a bowed stringed instrument was the old Celtic crwth, dating back to at least the sixth century AD; but the ancestor of most other bowed instruments was the medieval rebec, which probably made its way into Europe from the Middle East. Rebecs were made in a variety of sizes, the size of the instrument being directly related to its range of notes.

The first important family of bowed instruments were the viols, including closely related instruments like the viola d'amore. Viols had six strings, attached to tuning-pegs at the end of the neck and raised above the body of the instrument by a curved section of wood called a bridge. They also had frets (little raised strips of wood or metal, as in a guitar) inserted down the neck to aid stopping. They were normally placed on the player's knee (except for the larger versions, which were supported between the knees), the bow being drawn gently across their strings with the palm of the hand facing outwards. To modern ears, hearing them for the first time, viols may seem to produce a rather constrained, pinched sort of sound. But it is a sound that grows more attractive with acquaintance, and one that was perfectly suited to the polyphonic music popular in Renaissance times. It was not until about 1700 that the viol was finally superseded by the violin.

A violin, compared in shape and construction to a viol, has a longer, narrower neck, higher shoulders to the body and a rounded back. Most important of all, its strings (four in number) are tighter strung and supported by a stronger, more rounded bridge. From the start, these features, taken in conjunction with new methods of using the bow, gave the violin a brighter tone and stronger musical 'attack'; and further developments, notably in the lengthening of the neck and strengthening of the bow, improved these qualities. Playing styles for the instrument have also changed. In earlier days it was often pressed against the performer's chest rather than tucked under the chin, which did not give him such quick control over the instrument. The viola, cello and double-bass are, in all important respects, larger versions of the violin, giving to

Below: French gentleman of Louis XIV's time playing a bass viol, sometimes called in Italian *viola da gamba* because it was placed between the legs like a cello.
Right: Fine grouping of the violin family, from a nineteenth-century musical manual.

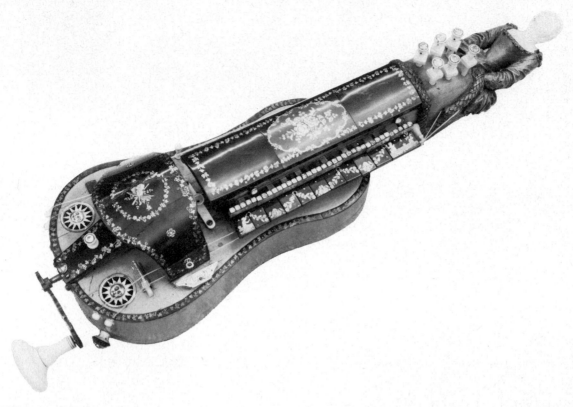

Beautifully made eighteenth-century hurdy-gurdy from France.

each a successively lower-pitched range of notes; but there is also a difference of thickness, and sometimes of material, in the strings, from one instrument to the next, and this too has its effect on pitch and tone.

The home of the violin was Italy, and the earliest models date from about the middle of the sixteenth century. The first great period of production was centred on the town of Cremona and the craftsmanship of several families of instrument-makers—the Stradivaris, Guarneris and Amatis. The first generation of important composers for the violin were also Italians—Corelli, Torelli, Vivaldi. Since the time of Bach and Handel, the violin family have provided the foundation of orchestral sound, being also numerically the largest section of almost any orchestra. As solo instruments, the violin and cello have been most popular with composers, though the viola has had its champions, including Berlioz, Hindemith (who was a viola player) and Walton. In chamber music, the beautifully

balanced combination of the string quartet—two violins, viola and cello—has inspired some of the greatest music from composers as different as Haydn, Mozart, Beethoven, Bartók and Shostakovich.

Two interesting variants of the bowed stringed instrument group are the tromba marina, which was a very tall one-stringed instrument, and the hurdy-gurdy. In the hurdy-gurdy a set of strings is laid across one segment of a wheel. The player turns the handle of the wheel, which activates the strings, while stopping them with his other hand to produce different notes. The continuous motion of the wheel against the strings produces a droning effect. There are medieval prints which show very large hurdy-gurdies being laid across the laps of two men, one turning the wheel, the other stopping the strings. Other varieties of the instrument have been elaborately constructed with a set of keys for the player to depress in order to stop the strings more easily than by manual control.

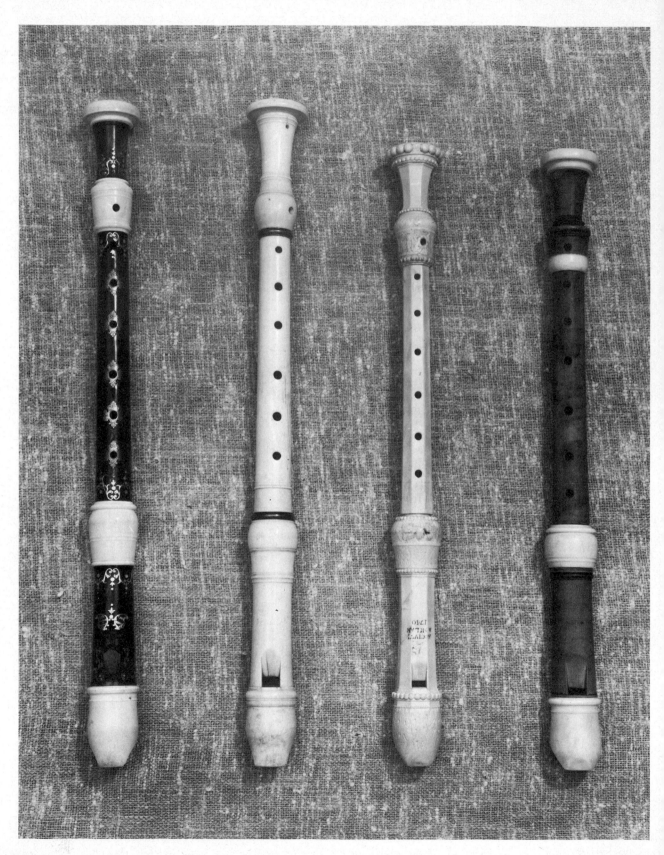

Woodwind Instruments

Woodwind instruments were at one time all actually made of wood. Today, some instruments classed as 'woodwind' are, in fact, made of metal, and the real distinction between woodwind and brass instruments lies not in their materials but in their design and methods of playing.

The basis of a woodwind instrument is either a tube which the player blows across or into at an angle in order to start the column of air inside vibrating, or a tube which amplifies and modifies the vibrations of a thin reed attached to one end. The other distinctive feature shared by virtually all woodwind instruments is that they have holes along the side of the tube, which the player covers or uncovers to alter the effective playing length of the instrument and so obtain notes of different pitch. It is possible to produce more than one note on any wind instrument just by blowing harder and so obtaining different notes in the basic harmonic series; but without the holes in a woodwind instrument the range of notes would be very limited and uncertain.

The recorder, very popular in Renaissance times, is a relatively simple woodwind instrument of the first type described above. The flute (like its smaller, higher-pitched companion the piccolo) is another which requires the player to blow across a mouthpiece, to activate the column of air inside the tube. As with early types of harp, so there are many ancient Egyptian pictures of flute-players. Some are shown holding the instrument downwards and blowing across one end. Others are playing the much more common transverse flute, holding the instrument sideways and blowing into a mouthpiece in its side. The modern type of flute owes its existence to the nineteenth-century German flute-player

Facing page: Four treble recorders of the eighteenth and nineteenth centuries. The one on the left is Italian, veneered with tortoiseshell and inlaid with gold pique and mother of pearl.
Right: Early eighteenth-century English flute, made of ebony and mounted in silver.
Far right: Italian oboe of the early eighteenth century.

Theobald Boehm. Before his time the positioning of the holes in the side was limited by the ability of the player to cover them with his fingers. Boehm re-designed the instrument, placing holes in the best position from the point of view of its own acoustics, at the same time making them possible to cover and uncover without great difficulty by a system of keys and levers. The pure, sometimes melancholy, sometimes rather sensual sound of the flute (especially in its lower registers) has always attracted musicians. The instrument was very popular in the eighteenth century, Frederick the Great of Prussia being an enthusiast. In orchestral music there is a prominent part for the flute in the scherzo of Mendelssohn's incidental music to *A Midsummer Night's Dream*, and the famous flute solo that opens Debussy's *Prélude à l'Après-midi d'un faune*.

The oboe's ancestors were the shawms, pommers and curtalls of the Middle Ages and Renaissance period. Its immediate predecessor was an instrument called, in French, *hautbois* ('loud wood'). The instrument as we know it today emerged during the latter part of the eighteenth century, in the time of Haydn and Mozart. It is classed as a double-reed instrument, having two thin narrow reeds which form the actual mouthpiece and vibrate against each other. Modern versions are equipped with keys and levers for the operation of the holes, based on the Boehm system. In orchestral music, the slightly larger, deeper-toned *cor anglais* ('English horn', though, confusingly, it has nothing specially to do with England and is not a horn) has tended to steal the limelight in solo passage work, the best-known example being the long opening theme to Berlioz's *Carnaval Romain* overture. Richard Strauss, however, composed a fine oboe concerto.

Closely related to the oboe (using a double reed) but with a distinctive sound of its own is the bassoon. One of its ancestors was the racket, in which the long tube of the instrument was coiled up inside a cylindrical box for convenient handling. A consort of rackets (a set of differently sized instruments) sounds rather like a group of melodious bees. The Italian word for bassoon, *fagotto*, meaning 'bundle', is a rather uncomplimentary way of describing how the long tube of the instrument is bent round itself. Its rather pawky tone in the middle registers has tended to cast the bassoon in a comic role in the orchestra, as in Dukas's light-hearted symphonic poem *L'Apprenti sorcier*. It can, however, be made to sound very forlorn, as it does at the beginning of

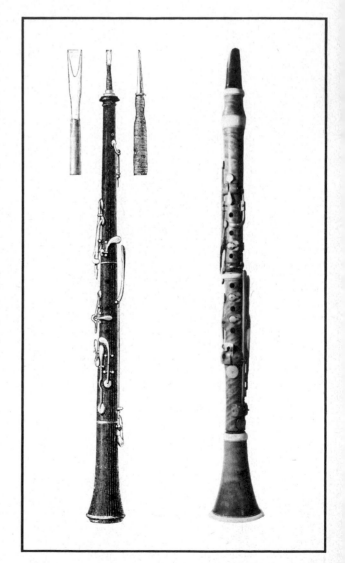

Right: French oboe (*hautbois*) of the late nineteenth century.
Far right: Clarinet of pear wood, with ivory rings and brass keys, made in England about 1840.

Tchaikovsky's 'Pathétique' Symphony, or bleak and desolate, as at the beginning of Stravinsky's *The Rite of Spring*. The bassoon can reach quite low notes. The more recently invented double-bassoon, or contra-bassoon, can play a whole octave lower and so plunge down to the very depths of orchestral sound. Ravel uses it to portray the beast in the Beauty and the Beast movement of his *Mother Goose* suite.

Though there were earlier woodwind instruments similar to it, the clarinet started life very much in its own right at around the beginning of the eighteenth century. It has a single reed which vibrates against the mouthpiece. The modern

Albrecht Dürer's famous engraving of a bagpiper, dated 1514.

instrument is equipped with levers and keys for the holes, again based on the Boehm system. It exists in various forms, tuned to particular keys, but the only variant with a real difference is the bass clarinet, which looks a little like a saxophone, and produces a dark, sinewy tone. Mozart, inspired by the playing of Anton Stadler, was the first composer to write great music for the clarinet—his Clarinet Quintet (K581) and Clarinet Concerto (K622). He also had a great affection for the deeper-toned basset horn (again, it has no connection with a true horn). Brahms and Weber have been two other outstanding composers for the clarinet. It has also figured prominently in jazz, in the hands of such famous instrumentalists as Sidney Bechet, Woody Herman, Benny Goodman and Artie Shaw. Generally the instrument has an open, easy sound, but in its upper registers it can sound quite frightening. Richard Strauss uses it in this way in his symphonic poem *Till Eulenspiegel* to depict the hero being strung up on a gallows.

The saxophone is generally classed as a woodwind instrument, because it has a reed and a woodwind-type arrangement of holes operated by levers and keys, although the tube itself is fashioned more like that of a brass instrument. It was invented by the Belgian Adolphe Sax in the last century, originally to add power to the woodwind section of French military bands. A few composers, notably Bizet and Vaughan Williams, have included passages for it in their orchestral music; and a small group of saxophones (made to different sizes—soprano, tenor, alto) can sound charming. But the instrument really came into its own in the field of jazz and dance music. Some of the greatest jazz players have been saxophonists—Charlie Parker, Lester Young, Coleman Hawkins, Gerry Mulligan, Stan Getz.

The bagpipes have long been associated with Scotland, but are one of the most ancient and widely distributed of woodwind-type instruments. The most distinctive feature of bagpipes is the bag or sack (traditionally made from the bladder or stomach of a sheep or goat) which acts as a reservoir for air. The player blows into this (or in some cases supplies it with a pair of bellows) then directs the air into a set of small pipes equipped with some kind of reed. The bagpipes probably originated somewhere in Asia, thousands of years ago. They are still found, in various forms, in many parts of the Middle East and Europe. The celebrated Scottish Highland bagpipes are a powerful instrument with a strong, strident tone, best heard in the open air. Other types, such as the Northumbrian pipes, have a much gentler, more mellifluous tone.

Brass Instruments

Brass instruments (usually but not always made of that metal) operate in quite a different way from woodwind instruments. The player presses his lips to one end of the metal tube and spits into the instrument. It is possible to obtain a note from a metal tube by blowing straight into it in the manner described, but all brass instruments are fitted with a cup- or funnel-shaped mouthpiece which allows the player much greater control over the pitch and tone. At the other end they are characterized by the way the tube opens out into what is called the bell.

Trumpets, the brass instruments most people first think of, have changed very little in their basic musical character for thousands of years. A type of trumpet found in the tomb of the Egyptian pharaoh Tutankhamun has the same fundamentally high, clear, penetrating sound as any trumpet heard today. This quality traditionally gave the trumpet an important role in signalling and in military operations, where it could be clearly heard above the sound of battle. Its bright, silvery tone also made it ideal for ceremonial fanfares. In the eighteenth century composers like Bach and Handel sometimes wrote very high-pitched trumpet parts, called clarino parts, requiring specialized skill on the instruments of their day. Until the nineteenth century the trumpet consisted of one long tube, extending in a straight line, or bent round itself for easier handling. In this form the player could extract from it only the basic notes of its natural harmonics. The famous trumpet call in Beethoven's *Leonora no 3* overture demonstrates this

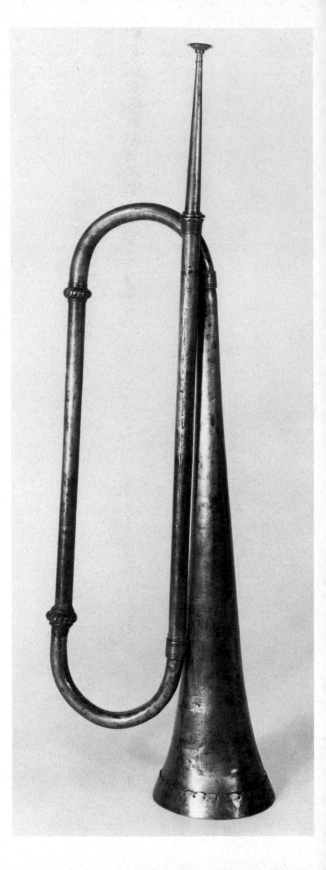

classic type of trumpet playing. During the last century, however, it was equipped with piston-operated valves to cut off or add sections to its playing length, thus greatly extending its range of notes. The bugle, smaller in size and without valves, and the cornet, with valves, are closely related to the standard trumpet. This century the trumpet has flourished in jazz, in the hands of such widely different musicians as Louis Armstrong, Dizzy Gillespie and Miles Davis; while the cornet, with its rounder tone, was 'Bix' Beiderbecke's favoured instrument.

The trombone is easily recognizable by its sliding valve mechanism, which shortens or increases the playing length of the instrument at will. In Renaissance and Baroque times it was known in England as the sackbut. The instrument has a full, rounded tone. It was much used in church music up to the eighteenth century. Mozart was one of the first to use trombones in the orchestra, in his opera *Don Giovanni*. Beethoven was the first to use them in a symphony (his Fifth). As with the trumpet, so the trombone has figured prominently this century in jazz, through the talents of Edward 'Kid' Ory, Jack Teagarden and swing band leaders Tommy Dorsey and Glenn Miller.

The horn, called in full the French horn, is basically rounded in shape, with a very wide bell. An ancient ancestor was the Scandinavian lur,

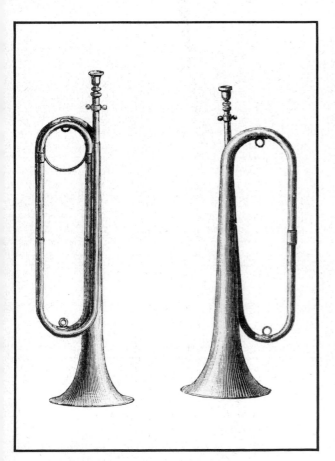

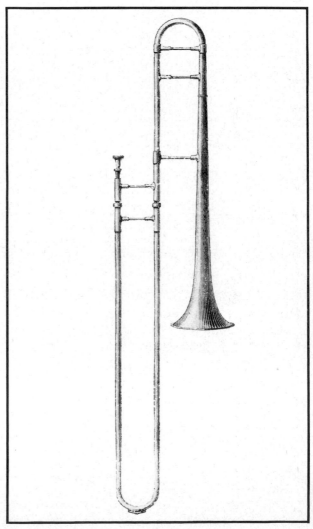

Facing page: Nineteenth-century 'natural' trumpet (i.e. without valves or crooks) from India. Note the relatively narrow 'bell'.
Above: Trumpet (left) and bugle, illustrated in a nineteenth-century manual.
Right: Nineteenth-century trombone with its familiar sliding valve.

Eighteenth-century engraving showing the manufacture of hunting horns. The craftsman at the back is filling a tube with molten lead to soften the metal and allow it to be fashioned into its circular shape.

made of bronze, but the horn as we think of it started off as a hunting instrument, and its romantic association with woods and fields is enhanced by its rather haunting, mellow tones. The old hunting horn consisted simply of a coiled tube, and like early trumpets was only capable of sounding the notes of its harmonic series. In the eighteenth century horns were provided with detachable sections called crooks. By adding or removing a crook the player altered the playing length of his instrument, so changing its harmonic range from one key to another. By the middle of the nineteenth century, crooks were superseded by piston valves, giving the horn, like the valve trumpet, much greater melodic freedom. The horn is the oldest brass instrument to have a regular place in the orchestra, and has been given more prominence than others. Mozart and Richard Strauss (whose father was a horn player) have written fine concertos for it. Famous horn solos in larger orchestral works

occur in the slow movement of Tchaikovsky's Fifth Symphony, and at the opening of Richard Strauss's *Till Eulenspiegel*. Berlioz also makes very imaginative use of the horn to suggest the tolling of a bell in the slow movement of his 'Harold in Italy' Symphony. Horns have also been used with great effect in ensemble work, as by Beethoven in the trio section to the scherzo of his 'Eroica' Symphony and by Wagner to depict King Mark's departure for the hunt in *Tristan und Isolde*.

In the modern orchestra the tuba is the deepest-toned brass instrument in regular use—a large, hefty instrument with an exceedingly wide bell and large, conical-bored tube equipped with piston valves, which the player rests on his lap, bell facing upwards. Like the double bass, the tuba almost always plays a supporting role in orchestral music, though Vaughan Williams wrote a concerto for it. Very similar is the euphonium, used in many military and brass bands.

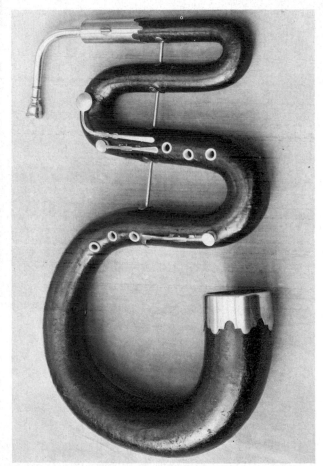

Tubas constructed in a circular fashion are called helicons, a particular example being the sousaphone, named after the American military band leader and composer Sousa. The sousaphone was also included in many early jazz bands, later being replaced by a string bass. The so-called Wagner tuba, designed by the composer for use in some of his music dramas, is, in fact, closer to a horn in construction and sound.

A now obsolete but interesting variant of a brass instrument is the appropriately named serpent. This was related to an even earlier type of wind instrument called the cornett which had a wooden, or sometimes ivory, tube with holes (like a woodwind instrument) but a small, cup-shaped mouthpiece like brass instruments. The serpent itself was made of either wood or metal (and usually covered with leather). It was popular both in church and in military bands, up until about the middle of the last century.

Wind bands generally have a long and interesting history. In the eighteenth and nineteenth centuries they usually consisted of oboes, clarinets, bassoons and horns, and inspired a few really great pieces of music (called *Harmoniemusik* in German), notably Mozart's wind serenades in B flat (K361) and in C minor (K388). Gounod also wrote a very attractive 'Petite Symphonie' for wind band.

Top: Nineteenth-century horn with a beautifully decorated 'bell'.
Above: A well-preserved example of the serpent.

115

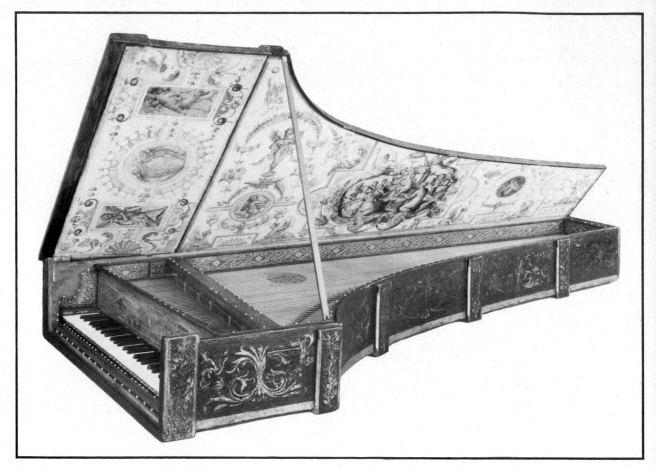

Magnificently decorated Italian harpsichord dated 1574.

Keyboard Instruments

A keyboard—the arrangement of levers or keys that activate the source of sound—is what links together a variety of instruments that might otherwise be variously classed as stringed instruments, wind or percussion.

The largest group of stringed keyboard instruments were the various forms of harpsichord. Their construction was based on that of much simpler instruments like the psaltery and dulcimer, which had a set of strings stretched over a sounding-board (i.e. resonator). Depression of the keys operated a device called a jack which plucked the strings. The virginal was the simplest type of harpsichord. At one time the name was fancifully believed to be connected with Elizabeth I (the 'Virgin Queen'), since the instru-

ment was very popular during her reign. The much more likely origin is the Latin word *virga* meaning a rod or jack, which forms an important part of its mechanism. Similar to it was the spinet. Both these instruments had their strings positioned horizontally along the length of the keyboard, or at a slight angle to it. The big difference with the true harpsichord was the placing of the strings in a direct line away from the keyboard. This difference in design gave the harpsichord more strength and volume of sound than the virginal and spinet. The most famous manufacturers of harpsichords were the Ruckers family of Antwerp during the seventeenth century. Bach and Handel, Couperin and Rameau all wrote great keyboard music for the instrument. Earlier this century such music was often

A modern Steinway concert grand piano.

played on a piano, but, with a revival of interest in the harpsichord, it is today again played on the instrument for which it was written.

The other stringed keyboard instrument, dating back like the harpsichords to Renaissance times, was the clavichord. This was equipped with a mechanism which struck the strings instead of plucking them, and for this reason can be considered the forerunner of the piano. What made the mechanism of the piano a real technical advance was the fact that the hammer struck the string and immediately bounced off again, leaving the string free to vibrate. Its inventor was the Italian Bartolommeo Cristofori, in about the year 1710. He called his early models incorporating this mechanism *gravicembalo col piano e forte* ('harpsichord with softness and loudness') to em-

phasize their new and greater dynamic range. The name became shortened in time to *piano-forte*, and then to *piano*—'soft'. In fact, it took the remainder of the eighteenth century for the piano to supersede the harpsichord, and nearly another hundred years—that is, up to about 1900—for it to emerge as the instrument we know today. Important landmarks in its development were the introduction of more strings and a wider keyboard; and the introduction of the upright piano (i.e. one with vertically placed strings) in about 1800 by the American manufacturer John Hawkins of Philadelphia. Of even greater significance was Hawkins's use of an iron frame which allowed the strings to be held in a far higher degree of tension and so to be capable of producing a fuller, stronger tone when hit.

Other famous piano manufacturers have been John Broadwood of London, Pleyel of Paris, Bösendorfer of Vienna, Bechstein of Berlin, and Steinway of New York. From about the middle of the eighteenth century many of the greatest composers have written for the piano of their time—C.P.E. and J.C. Bach, Haydn, Mozart, Beethoven, Schumann, Chopin, Brahms, Liszt, Debussy and Ravel—thus providing it with the richest, most varied musical literature of any single instrument.

The organ is basically a set of pipes—usually of two types, the so-called flue pipes constructed something like a whistle, and the more complex reed pipes—attached to a reservoir of air called a wind chest. Depression of the keys operates a mechanism that allows air from the wind chest to blow into the corresponding pipes and so produce notes. The history of the instrument dates back to the second or third century BC, and to the invention of an intriguing kind of organ called a hydraulus. This, as its Greek name suggests, involved the use of water to pump air into the wind chest and maintain it at a fairly constant pressure. The Egyptians, Greeks and Romans all had versions of the hydraulus, and several representations of it have survived, though exactly how it worked is now something of a mystery.

The earliest organs of the Christian era, dating from about the ninth century, were not really keyboard instruments, because slots of wood called sliders had to be pulled or pushed to control the passage of air into the pipes. A very large organ of about this time, installed in Winchester Cathedral, apparently needed over fifty men to operate it—to work both the sliders and the giant bellows supplying it with air. For some time to come organs remained rather clumsy affairs, early keyboards consisting of broad wooden keys which needed to be thumped hard with the fist to make them work. During the later Middle Ages and Renaissance periods there were two varieties of the instrument: the portative organ, which was small enough to be carried about, and the larger positive organ.

Organs dating from the seventeenth century set the pattern for future development, with one or more keyboards (or manuals), an additional pedal board of long wooden levers (a German invention), and stops contained in panels by the side of the keyboards which allowed the player to select whole sets of pipes with particular sound qualities. The German Silbermann family, well known to Bach, made some of the finest organs of the Baroque period (as well as harpsichords and clavichords). In the nineteenth century, as a symbol of the wealth and advancing technology of the Industrial Revolution, some mammoth instruments were made. Earlier this century there was also the cinema organ, operated electronically, which included many novel sound effects. In terms of serious organ building, there has been a return this century to the fairly modest size of the Baroque instruments. Bach's organ

Engraving of a fifteenth-century positive organ. Note the bellows.

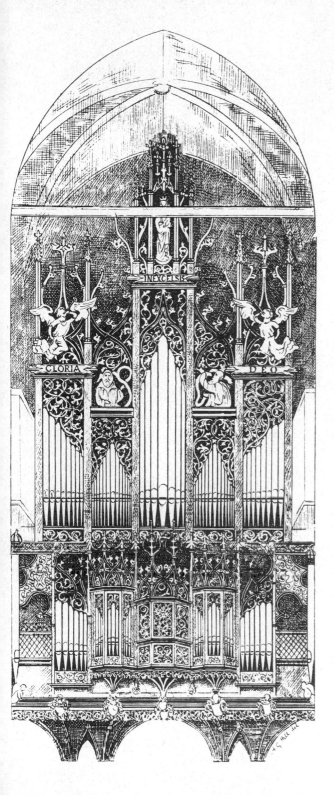

The splendid sixteenth-century organ in the Marienkirche, Lübeck, where Buxtehude was organist (see page 130).

music was the greatest written for the instrument. For over a hundred years after his death the organ was neglected by most composers, but this century more important music has been added to its repertory, especially by composers like Messiaen, who have added to the long tradition of French organ music.

There are a variety of instruments belonging to what is called the reed-organ family. Usually they have no pipes, the sound coming directly from freely vibrating reeds. An early example, dating from Renaissance times, was a very small kind of portable organ called a regal. One version of this, the Bible regal, could be opened and closed like a book. More recent members of this family include the mouth organ or harmonica, the accordion and concertina. There is also the harmonium with a keyboard and bellows pumped by the player's feet. None of these instruments has risen to great musical heights, but Dvořák was one composer who had a soft spot for the harmonium, while the American Larry Adler has shown how much fine music can be played on the harmonica.

Mechanical Instruments

These operate without direct human control. In the past they have usually been driven by some sort of clockwork, while an apparatus known as 'barrel-and-pin' has been most widely used as the actual agent of their performance. This is an accurate enough description of a barrel or cylinder carefully fitted with pegs or pins. As the barrel revolves the pins activate the levers, pulleys, stops or other devices which control the source of sound. As long ago as the fourteenth century, the barrel-and-pin principle was applied to the chiming of bells. By the sixteenth century barrel-and-pin mechanisms were being installed in virginals and organs. Elizabeth I is reported to have sent the Sultan of Turkey a mechanical instrument of this kind which could play a continuous selection of pieces for nearly seven hours. The barrel-and-pin mechanism has been applied to musical clocks and to musical boxes. Here the revolving pattern of pins strikes a row of little metal bars, their graded length producing a range of notes. An interesting variant of this was the nineteenth-century polyphon, designed to play metal discs with a pattern of pins or notches inscribed on them. As the disc revolved, so the notches activated the striking of the tuned metal bars. The discs were detachable, so giving the owner a choice of music, and anticipating the idea of the modern record disc.

A newer method of mechanical production has been the perforated roll, usually made of specially stiffened paper. Instead of pins or pegs, the perforations in the roll operate the instrument pneumatically (that is, with the aid of air, or perhaps of steam). Most mechanical fairground steam organs, or calliopes, have worked on this principle. So have mechanical pianos, called pianolas or player pianos. In their case the perforated-roll technique proved efficient enough for some great pianists to 'cut' rolls which would accurately reproduce their performance. Pianolas or other types of reproducing pianos usually have keyboards like any normal instrument, so that as the rolls are fed into them the individual keys, operated from within, move rather uncannily up and down as though at the command of some ghostly, unseen hand.

Some mechanical instruments have been very elaborate. Johann Maelzel, who produced an early type of metronome (a mechanical device using a sort of inverted pendulum to indicate tempo speeds), also invented the Panharmonicon, which was like a whole mechanical orchestra. Beethoven was friendly with Maelzel and composed his piece called *The Battle of Victoria* (also known, in the version for a normal orchestra, as the 'Battle Symphony') for the Panharmonicon.

The Voice

This is the instrument as old as humanity itself, but continually new. None of us needs to be told how to use it—we usually demonstrate this within moments of being born—but we can all get much more out of it with care and training. The voice cannot be directly compared with any man-made instrument. The source of its sound is in the larynx, in the front of the throat. Attached to the larynx are the vocal chords. These are membranes—a little over a centimetre long in an adult male, slightly less in women and children—which we automatically tighten when we wish to use our voice, so that the air we breathe out from the lungs and up the windpipe makes them vibrate and produce sound. Other parts of our anatomy—chest and neck, mouth and nose (including the sinus cavities above the nose)—then act as a complex resonator, amplifying and shaping the pitch and tone of our vocal chords. How differently these factors affect the voice can be understood by comparing the traditional Eastern way of singing, which is largely through the nose, with the Western tradition of opening the mouth wide.

The origins of song—using the word in this

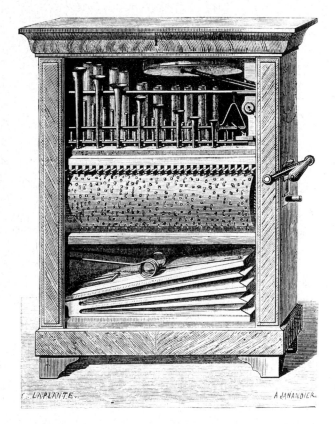

Small mechanically operated organ showing very clearly its barrel-and-pin mechanism. Note the percussive effects of bell and triangle.

The Westminster Abbey choir representing the age-old combination of boys' and men's voices.

context to include all kinds of chants, laments and war cries—is lost in history. People almost certainly used their voice in what might be considered some form of musical expression before they developed proper speech, and before they had invented any other instruments that we might recognize as such. As far as the beginnings of European or Western music are concerned, the voice played a far more important part than any other instrument for several hundred years—in the singing of church plainsong and other forms of chanting. And when church vocal music began to lose its lead during the late Middle Ages and the Renaissance, so opera, oratorio and song emerged to keep the voice in the forefront of music.

Musically, voices are classified according to their range of notes. In the case of women they are soprano (the highest-pitched), mezzo-soprano (half-soprano, or not quite so high) and contralto. In men the basic division is between tenor (the highest-pitched), baritone and bass. Boys' voices are considered differently, being defined as treble or alto. When they 'break' it means that the vocal chords are growing larger and tougher, together with the throat muscles and other related parts of the body. It is the musical sign of approaching manhood. In the past, when the church did not permit the use of women's voices, boys were sometimes castrated to deny them full manhood and so keep their voices unbroken. The object was to combine the

121

soprano tone with the power and control of a man's pair of lungs. Such singers—often very famous and successful—were known as castrati. It is, however, possible for a normal man to speak or sing in a falsetto voice (like a boy), and with care and training some male singers, called counter-tenors, can come very close to the sound of a true castrato.

These long-established divisions between different types of voice, male and female, are not so important in jazz, dance and pop music. This is partly because of the character of the music itself, and partly because since the 1920s nearly all such vocalists have used microphones as an essential part of their performance. Clever and creative use of the microphone allows them to project a vocal personality that is usually more important than the intrinsic nature or quality of their voice.

Cleo Laine, one of today's most versatile and attractive jazz vocalists.

Electrophonic Instruments

The microphone, as used by vocalists, is an example of the way the production of musical sound has been revolutionized during this century by electrical means. In the case of the microphone, an electrical device is being used in conjunction with an existing instrument—the voice. The partnership between a conventional instrument and electrical appliances has been developed in various other ways. In the Neo-Bechstein piano, for example, the strings of the instrument are set vibrating by the conventional use of hammers, but their vibrations are then picked up, amplified and modified electrically, the sound finally being delivered through loudspeakers. The Vierling violin is played in the usual way, but is similarly wired for sound. In the last thirty years the guitar has become the most popular of such electrically-aided instruments, bearing little resemblance to a 'classical' guitar, because its shape and size have relatively little to do with its sound reproduction.

True electrophonic instruments are those in which the source of sound is also electronic. An early and well-known example is the American-designed Hammond Organ, which has a conventional keyboard, but no pipes. The sounds are created, modified and amplified entirely by electronic means. In the case of the Hammond Organ and similar designs, the resulting sounds still resemble those of an existing instrument. Other electrophonic instruments, whose sound source is usually some type of electrical valve oscillator or oscillators, can produce sounds which are radically different from those heard on any conventional instrument. Well before the Second World War there was already a wide range of such devices. One of these was the *Ondes Martenot*, or Martenot Waves, named after its French inventor Maurice Martenot. This is activated by a normal keyboard, but produces a succession of notes which are remarkably pure, rather unearthly in tone, and belonging to a realm of sound beyond that of normal musical acoustics.

Since the war electrophonic music has become important to many composers. The magnetic

One of the most up-to-date electronic synthesizers in use today.
This one is called an EMS Synthi 100.

recording tape has enabled them to take quite ordinary sounds and transform them, by a process of play-backs, re-recordings and cutting, into the most extraordinary sound patterns. Even more significant has been the arrival on the scene of the synthesizer. The word 'synthesize' means to bring together, to build up, and the apparatus can start with basic sound oscillations and build them up, by the most complex electronic analysis of wave patterns and overtones, to imitate conventional instruments, or to create sounds right outside the province of normal experience. Electrophonic engineers and composers who use synthesizers need to know about the scientific 'anatomy' of sound—of the action and interaction of overtones and harmonics, of the physical properties of different types of sound wave, and of the so-called 'decay' of sound. Just as a synthesizer can build up sounds, so it can take them apart, filtering them and stripping them layer by layer of their overtones and harmonics, until there is nothing left but the hiss known as 'white' sound. Thus can one person create a universe of sound, as astonishing as any trip into space, and dissolve it again, just with the touch of his fingers.

Musicians

Adam de la Halle
(about 1231–88).
Most famous of the poet-musicians called *trouvères* who lived in France during the Middle Ages. He wrote a play with music called the *Jeu de' Robin et Marion*, which anticipated certain kinds of opera by nearly five hundred years.

Albéniz, Isaac (1860–1909).
Spanish composer and pianist. As a child prodigy he studied with Liszt, then travelled widely and lived mainly in London and Paris. As a composer Albéniz made great use of the traditional rhythms and harmonies of his own country and was an important figure in the Spanish nationalist school of music. His compositions include a set of piano pieces, each representing a different region of Spain, called collectively *Iberia*; and a very popular Tango.

Armstrong, Louis 'Satchmo'
(1900–71).
American jazz trumpeter, whose early career sounds very like the early history of jazz itself. He joined Edward 'Kid' Ory's New Orleans band in 1918, then played for a period on Mississippi riverboats before joining Joe 'King' Oliver's band in Chicago. Armstrong later became a great show-business personality, appearing in many films, so winning a big new audience for his kind of 'traditional' jazz.

Arne, Thomas Augustine
(1710–78).
English composer, mainly of operas and other stage works with music. These are rarely performed today, but he remains famous as composer of the song 'Rule, Britannia' (first heard as a part of one of his masques). His son Michael wrote another song which is still popular, 'The Lass with the Delicate Air'.

Bach, Johann Sebastian
(1685–1750).
German composer and organist. Born in Eisenach, Thuringia (now in East Germany), he held various posts as organist, choirmaster and director of music, the last of these being at the school and church of St Thomas (*Thomasschule*) in Leipzig, where he died. Bach won great fame as an organist, but as a composer he was not highly rated by most of his contemporaries and his music was neglected for many years afterwards. Now he is recognized, with Handel, as the last great composer of the Baroque period and the last great master of polyphonic styles of music. He composed in virtually every form of his time, except opera, his work falling into three main categories: (1) compositions for the organ—fantasias, chorales, preludes and fugues; (2) orchestral and instrumental music—the 'Brandenburg' Concertos and other concerto-style works (some being arrangements of music by other composers), the

Forty-eight Preludes and Fugues for the keyboard (also called *Das wolhtemperierte Clavier*), the 'Goldberg' Variations, numerous suites and partitas, *The Musical Offering* (for Frederick the Great of Prussia) and *The Art of Fugue* (which exists in several versions); (3) choral works—nearly 300 church cantatas (from one of which comes the well-known piece known as 'Jesu, Joy of Man's Desiring'), some secular cantatas (including the 'Coffee' Cantata), the Christmas Oratorio, St John and St Matthew Passions, and Mass in B minor. This immense output has been catalogued and indexed by the German scholar Wolfgang Schmieder, and individual works are now often quoted with their BWV number—*Bach Werke-Verzeichnis* ('Index of Bach's Works'). Of Bach's twenty children by his two marriages, three of his sons became important musical figures in their own right. Wilhelm Friedemann (1710–84), the eldest son, was a highly gifted man and composer of much fine organ and keyboard music, but was not successful and died in poverty. Carl Philipp Emanuel (1714–88), for some years court musician to Frederick the Great, wrote symphonies and sonatas in the new Classical style of his time, his keyboard pieces being especially interesting for the way they mark the change in style from composition for the harpsichord to that for the much newer piano. Johann Christian

(1735–82) settled in London, henceforth being known as the 'English Bach' or 'London Bach'. He wrote operas, also symphonies and piano concertos in the new Classical style, and gave some lessons to Mozart when he visited London as a child.

Balakirev, Mily (1837–1910). Russian composer and founder-member of the group of Russian nationalist composers known as 'The Five'. He wrote two symphonies, a symphonic poem, and much piano music including the fantasy *Islamey* which is strongly Asiatic in mood. There is an orchestral version of this.

Barber, Samuel (born 1910). American composer whose music is generally quite traditional and lyrical in style. His works include two sym-phonies, the opera *Vanessa* (with a libretto by his American colleague Gian-Carlo Menotti), the ballet *Medea* and the very well-known Adagio for Strings (originally the slow movement of a string quartet).

Bartók, Béla (1881–1945). Hungarian composer whose intensive study of Hungarian and Romanian folk music largely shaped his own very original style and made him a major figure of twentieth-century music. His works include the opera *Duke Bluebeard's Castle*, the ballet *The Miraculous Mandarin*, three piano concertos, two violin concertos, Music for Strings, Percussion and Celesta, Concerto for Orchestra, six string quartets, and much music for the piano, notably *Mikrokosmos* (over 150 pieces of graded technical difficulty) and the suite *Out of Doors*. Soon after the outbreak of the Second World War Bartók emigrated to the United States, but despite his fame his last years were sad and lonely ones.

Basie, William 'Count' (born 1904). American jazz musician and, from the 1930s to the 1960s, one of the leading figures of 'big band' or 'mainstream' jazz. His bands, usually directed by him from the piano, were famed for their musical precision and 'attack' and strong rhythmic drive. His early composition 'One O'Clock Jump' also became his signature tune.

Below: Count Basie in concert

Béla Bartók

Beethoven, Ludwig van
(1770–1827).

German composer. He was born in Bonn but as a young man settled permanently in Vienna (where he died). His career as a pianist was ruined by approaching deafness, and from then on he concentrated on composition, dramatically enlarging the Classical forms of the symphony, concerto, string quartet and sonata and greatly increasing the expressive power of music. By his fiercely independent spirit, and despite deafness and frequent ill-health, he also raised the stature of the artist in society. Through his work, attitudes and way of life Beethoven can thus be seen as the great dividing figure between the Classical eighteenth century and the Romantic nineteenth century, and his influence on music has been enormous. His principal works are: nine symphonies—no 1 in C major (opus 21), no 2 in D major (opus 36), no 3 in E flat ('Eroica', opus 55), no 4 in B flat (opus 60), no 5 in C minor (opus 67), no 6 in F major ('Pastoral', opus 68), no 7 in A major (opus 92), no 8 in F major (opus 93), no 9 in D minor ('Choral', opus 125); five piano concertos—no 5 in E flat (opus 73) being nicknamed 'Emperor'; Violin Concerto in D (opus 61); the opera *Fidelio* (originally called *Leonora*); Mass in D (*Missa Solemnis*, opus 123); overture and incidental music to Goethe's play *Egmont*; sixteen string quartets, including the six of opus 18, the three of opus 59 (known as the 'Rassumovsky' Quartets), and the group composed at the end of his life, plus the separately published *Grosse Fuge* (opus 133); thirty-two piano sonatas, including no 8 in C minor ('Pathétique', opus 13), no 14 in C sharp minor (opus 27 no 2, nick-named 'Moonlight'), no 21 in C major ('Waldstein', opus 53), no 23 in F minor ('Appassionata', opus 57), no 29 in B flat ('Hammerklavier', opus 106); also for the piano, the 'Diabelli' Variations (opus 120); and many other instrumental works.

Bix Beiderbecke

Beiderbecke, Leon Bismarck 'Bix' (1903–31).

American cornet player and one of the first great white jazz musicians. He played in several bands, including the Wolverines, and later with the Paul Whiteman band, winning acclaim for his flawless technique and lilting style. He also wrote a piano piece, 'In a Mist', which is notable for its Debussy-like harmonies.

Bellini, Vincenzo (1801–35).
Italian composer of operas in the *bel canto* style, including *I Puritani* ('The Puritans'), *La Sonnambula* ('The Sleepwalker') and *Norma* (a Druidic priestess in Roman Gaul).

Berg, Alban (1885–1935).
Austrian composer. He was a pupil of Schoenberg and developed twelve-tone methods of composition in his

own work, proving that they could be the basis for very expressive and beautiful music. He is best known today for his opera *Wozzeck* (about a poor, persecuted soldier) and his Violin Concerto (written on the death of a friend's daughter and bearing the dedication 'in memory of an angel').

Berlin, Irving (born 1888).
American song-writer, the son of Russian immigrants, whose real name was Israel Baline. His famous songs, many written for stage shows or films, include 'Alexander's Ragtime Band', 'I'm Dreaming of a White Christmas' and 'How Deep is the Ocean?'. He also wrote the music for the stage and film musical *Call me Madam*, and the patriotic song 'God Bless America'. He never learnt properly how to play the piano or read music.

Berlioz, Hector (1803–69).
French composer and major figure in the development of Romantic music. He studied music against his father's wishes, and from his days as a student in Paris had to struggle for his livelihood, never earning the recognition or the rewards he thought he deserved. The two principal features of his music are vivid orchestration (he wrote a book on the subject) and compositions on a very large scale (inspired by the great open-air ceremonies of the French Revolutionary period), though he could write with delicacy and restraint. His works include the *Symphonie Fantastique*; the symphony *Harold in Italy* (based on a poem by Byron and with a part for solo viola, originally intended for Paganini); the dramatic symphony for soloists, chorus and orchestra *Romeo and Juliet* (after Shakespeare); the dramatic cantata, sometimes staged as an opera, *La Damnation de Faust* (after Goethe); the oratorio *L'Enfance du Christ* ('Childhood of Christ'); a Requiem Mass; song-cycle, with orchestra, *Nuits d'Ete* ('Summer Nights'); and the concert overtures *Le Corsair* and *Le Carnaval Romain* (music taken from his opera *Benvenuto Cellini*). His greatest work for the stage, the opera *Les Troyens* ('The Trojans'), was never performed complete in his lifetime.

Bernart de Ventadorn
(about 1130–95).
One of the most famous of the troubadour poet-musicians of medieval Provence. He was much admired by Eleanor of Aquitaine, who invited him to England after her marriage to Henry II.

Bernstein, Leonard (born 1918).
American conductor (closely associated with the New York Philharmonic Orchestra), pianist, and composer of the symphonies called *Jeremiah* and *Age of Anxiety*. In a lighter, often jazz-inspired style he has also written the music to the ballet *Fancy Free* (later adapted for the film *On The Town*) and to the very successful stage and film musical *West Side Story* (which retells the story of *Romeo and Juliet* in a New York City setting). A very unusual work is his *Mass* for singers, players and dancers.

Leonard Bernstein

Binchois, Gilles (about 1400–60). Burgundian soldier, priest and chief composer at the court of Philip the Good in Dijon, best remembered today for his secular *chansons* (songs), often very expressive for their time.

Bizet, Georges (1838–75). French composer with a wonderful natural gift for melody and strong, bright orchestration, as heard in the incidental music he wrote to Daudet's play *L'Arlésienne* ('The Girl from Arles') and the suite *Jeux d'enfants* ('Children's Games'). He also wrote the operas *The Pearl Fishers* and *The Fair Maid of Perth* (based on the novel by Sir Walter Scott). His last opera, *Carmen* (the name of the Spanish gipsy heroine), has long been one of the most popular in the repertory. Tragically, Bizet died soon after the première, just before it became a real success. A Symphony in C, written when Bizet was only seventeen, is also a very popular piece of concert music.

Bliss, Sir Arthur (1891–1975). Master of the Queen's Music and composer of several works with interesting and unusual associations, notably the 'Colour' Symphony (which relates the mood of each movement to a particular colour) and the ballet *Checkmate* (based on a game of chess); also of music to the film *Things to Come*.

Bloch, Ernest (1880–1959). Swiss-born composer who settled in the United States, becoming an American citizen. His best-known pieces are those inspired by Jewish history and religion. They include the 'Israel' Symphony for voices and orchestra; *Avodath Hakodesh* ('Sacred Service') for baritone, chorus and orchestra; *Shelomo* ('Solomon') for cello and orchestra; and *Baal Shem* (the name of a seventeenth-century Hebrew leader) for violin and piano.

Boccherini, Luigi (1743–1805). Italian composer and cellist. He wrote symphonies, concertos and over 200 string quintets and quartets, similar in style and character to the music of his contemporary Haydn, but remembered today largely on the strength of a single minuet.

Borodin, Alexander (1833–87). Russian composer and member of the group of nationalist composers known as 'The Five'. He was also an eminent chemist and could spare little time for music. Some of the music he did write has become very popular, including the 'Polovtsian Dances' from his opera *Prince Igor* (completed by his colleague Rimsky-Korsakov); the symphonic poem *In the Steppes of Central Asia*; also two completed symphonies.

Boulez, Pierre (born 1925). French composer and conductor. As a composer he has developed Schoenberg's twelve-tone methods of composition, often applying mathematical principles to his work, and his music is considered to be 'advanced' in character. As a conductor he has also specialized in the music of Schoenberg and other twelve-tone composers, though he has won acclaim for his interpretations of Wagner, Debussy and Stravinsky. He is Director of the Centre for Acoustical Studies in Paris.

Boyce, William (1710–79). English organist and composer of stage music and songs, including the well-known patriotic song 'Heart of Oak', also of several symphonies in the early Classical style.

Brahms, Johannes (1833–97). German composer. He was born in Hamburg and as a young man received much help and encouragement from Robert and Clara Schumann. After Robert's death, Clara remained one of his very few close friends. Like Beethoven before him, he settled in Vienna, where he died. Although a fine pianist, Brahms gave most of his time to composition, combining Classical forms like the symphony and sonata with a more Romantic mood. His early works are generally large and serious in character, his later ones are far more relaxed, warm and mellow in spirit, and often of great harmonic and rhythmic subtlety. His output includes four symphonies—no 1 in C minor, no 2 in D major, no 3 in F major, no 4 in E minor; two piano concertos—no 2 in B flat being one of the grandest of all concertos, with four instead of the usual three movements; a violin concerto; a 'double' concerto for violin and cello; the orchestral Variations on the St Anthony Chorale (formerly thought to be a theme by Haydn); the *Academic Festival* and *Tragic* concert overtures; the choral *Ein deutsches Requiem* ('A German Requiem', based not on the Catholic Requiem Mass but on selected passages from the Lutheran Bible); sonatas and other instrumental chamber music works, notably three string quartets; many piano pieces and *Lieder* (Songs); also the popular Hungarian Dances.

Britten, Sir Benjamin (1913–76). English composer mainly of stage and vocal music, written in a fairly traditional but distinctive style that has had a wide appeal. His works include the operas *Peter Grimes* (based on a poem by George Crabbe and set on the Suffolk coast); *Billy Budd* (about the British navy of Nelson's time); *The Turn of the Screw* (after the ghost story by Henry James) and *Death in Venice* (based on the novel by Thomas Mann); 'Spring' Symphony for voices and orchestra (ending with 'Sumer is icumen in'); Variations and Fugue on a Theme of Purcell (*The Young Person's Guide to the Orchestra*); *Let's Make an Opera* and other works for children. Britten also founded the Aldeburgh Music Festival on the Suffolk coast, not far from his birthplace.

Sir Benjamin Britten

Bruch, Max (1838–1920).
German composer of operas, symphonies and other orchestral works—notably the Violin Concerto no 1 in G minor—written in a generally Romantic style.

Bruckner, Anton (1824–96).
Austrian organist and composer. His principal works are nine symphonies, whose rich orchestration and grand scale reflect his great love of Wagner's music—no 3 is dedicated to him, while Symphonies nos 7, 8 and 9 contain parts for the Wagner tuba; no 4 is named the 'Romantic'. An interesting oddity is an early symphony which is known as Symphony no 0. Bruckner, a devout Catholic, also composed three masses, a Requiem and a *Te Deum* (hymn of thanksgiving).

Bull, John (1563–1628).
English composer and organist, but specially noted today for his keyboard pieces for the virginals, one of which is thought to be the origin of 'God Save the Queen'.

Bülow, Hans Guido von (1830–94).
German pianist and conductor—one of the first to make his name primarily as a conductor on account of his exciting interpretations and concert-hall manner. He worked closely with Wagner for some years, and his wife Cosima (Liszt's daughter) left him for the composer.

Buxtehude, Diderik (1637–1707).
Danish organist and composer who worked for most of his life in Germany, so that he is better known as Dietrich Buxtehude. His playing and his organ music influenced Bach (who once walked nearly 200 miles to hear him play). Handel also visited him and admired his music.

Byrd, William (1543–1623).
English organist and composer who lived during the troubled religious times that led to the creation of the Church of England. Though a Catholic, he wrote music both for his own and for the Anglican Church; also renowned for his madrigals, keyboard pieces and other secular music. He and his older colleague Thomas Tallis were given a monopoly of music printing (then a new technique) by Elizabeth I.

Below: William Byrd

Anton Bruckner

Cage, John (born 1912).
American composer and important figure in twentieth-century musical thought. His idea of the 'Prepared Piano'—using objects placed between or over the strings—produced a startling new range of sounds. He also conceived of an extraordinary piece called *4'33"* (4 min 33 sec), during which time a pianist sits before a piano and makes certain gestures but does not play a single note. The idea is to draw the audience's attention to the multitude of sounds that still exist during periods of apparent silence.

Callas, Maria (1923–77).
Greek–American operatic soprano, whose original name was Kalogeropoulou. She was acclaimed especially for her singing of Italian opera—Bellini, Donizetti, Puccini—and for her very powerful stage presence.

Carissimi, Giacomo (1605–74).
Italian composer, important in musical history for his pioneer work in the field of oratorio. *Jephtha*, his most famous oratorio, served as a model for later composers.

Carter, Elliott (born 1908).
American composer who has been influenced by the so-called neo-Classical style of Stravinsky, and has also used serial methods of composition related to the twelve-tone techniques of Schoenberg. His works include the ballet *Minotaur* and a symphony.

Below: Enrico Caruso

Caruso, Enrico (1873–1921).
Italian operatic tenor who was one of the first serious musical artists to become a recording star (in the early days of acoustical recording) and achieved world-wide fame as a result.

Casals, Pau (1876–1973).
Spanish cellist, noted especially for his playing of Bach's music for unaccompanied cello, which he did much to revive. He held strong political views, exiling himself from Spain after Franco's victory in the Civil War, and founding the Prades music festival in southern France. As a Catalan nationalist he preferred the first name Pau to the Spanish Pablo.

Cavalli, Pietro Francesco (1620–76).
Italian composer who worked with Monteverdi in Venice for some time and wrote more than thirty operas of his own.

Chabrier, Emmanuel (1841–94).
French pianist, conductor and composer. His rhapsody *España*, inspired by a visit to Spain, is a favourite orchestral showpiece, and exuberant in spirit like much of his other music, though later in life he suffered badly from depression.

Chaliapin, Feodor Ivanovich (1875–1938).
Russian operatic bass, noted above all for his moving performances of the title role in Mussorgsky's opera *Boris Godunov*.

Charpentier, Marc-Antoine (about 1634–1704)
French composer of church music, also of operas and ballets. Like Lully, he worked with Molière and other dramatists of the time.

Chávez, Carlos (born 1899)
Mexican composer who has studied his country's folk music and developed a national style. One of his works includes native Mexican instruments and is named after the Aztec god of music.

Luigi Cherubini

Cherubini, Luigi (1760–1842).

Italian composer who worked for most of his life in Paris, where he was director of the Conservatory and one of the most eminent musical figures of his time. He wrote several successful operas, and Beethoven greatly admired his work. Today, the only piece of his music which is widely known is the overture to his opera *Iphigénie en Aulide*.

Chopin, Frédéric Francois (1810–49).

Polish-French composer and pianist. He was born in Poland, and though he spent most of his adult life in Paris remained intensely patriotic towards the country of his birth. Chopin composed almost exclusively for the piano. His music is often Romantically expressive, but always beautifully fashioned and refined, and marvellously suited to his chosen instrument. He wrote two early piano concertos, primarily for his own use on concert tours, and three sonatas; otherwise his output consists of groups of fairly short individual pieces—polonaises and mazurkas (based on traditional types of Polish dance), studies (*études*) which highlight different aspects of piano technique, preludes, ballades, waltzes, scherzos, impromptus and nocturnes. Some of these pieces have been given fanciful nicknames, not by Chopin, e.g. the 'Revolutionary' and 'Winter Wind' studies, the 'Raindrop' Prelude, 'Minute' Waltz. The ballet *Les Sylphides* is based on his music. Chopin is also famous for his love affair with George Sand, assumed name of the writer Aurore Dudevant. He died of consumption like many others in the past.

Cimarosa, Domenico (1749–1801).

Italian composer of over sixty operas, including *Il Matrimonio segreto* ('The Secret Marriage'), a comic opera similar in style to some of Mozart's. Cimarosa was a very successful man, holding important posts in Vienna and St Petersburg.

Clementi, Muzio (1752–1832).

Italian pianist and composer. He was a pioneer composer of piano music, including a collection of studies called *Gradus ad Parnassum* ('Steps to Parnassus'—the mountain which in Greek mythology was the home of the Muses). He settled in London where he also manufactured pianos.

Coleridge-Taylor, Samuel (1875–1912).

English composer—though his father was West African—of several musically picturesque works, notably a group of cantatas collectively called *Hiawatha*, inspired by Longfellow's poem of Red Indian life.

Copland, Aaron (born 1900).

American composer who has done much for the cause of his country's music by basing many of his own compositions on American folk songs and dances, also jazz, or on scenes from American life. His works include the ballets *Billy the Kid*, *Rodeo* and *Appalachian Spring*, the orchestral piece *El Salón México*, and *A Lincoln Portrait* for narrator and orchestra. He has also written symphonies, a clarinet concerto specially for Benny Goodman, and some music for films.

Corelli, Arcangelo (1653–1713).

Italian composer and violinist. He was one of the first great composers of music for the violin family of instruments, doing much to establish the concerto grosso form of writing for strings. Handel was greatly influenced by his style.

Above: Aaron Copland

Left: François Couperin

Couperin, François (1668–1733).
French composer, harpsichordist and
organist, sometimes called Couperin
le grand ('the Great') to distinguish
him from other members of his very
musical family. He served at the court
of Louis XIV, writing many organ
and choral works for use in church;
but is best remembered for his
harpsichord compositions, mostly
written in groups called *ordres* or
suites (some with picturesque titles)
which are among the finest
instrumental pieces of the Baroque
period. He wrote a book on
keyboard technique, now a valuable
guide to the playing styles of his
time.

Czerny, Carl (1791–1857).
Austrian composer, and key figure in
the history of piano music. He took
lessons from Beethoven, was, in turn,
a teacher of Liszt, and wrote a large
number of studies for the instrument.

Dallapiccola, Luigi (1904–75). Italian composer who followed Schoenberg's twelve-tone methods of composition, seeking to extend the appreciation of such music in a wide range of compositions, including operas, piano pieces and songs.

Davis, Miles (born 1926). American jazz trumpeter who developed, during the 1950s, a very 'cool' ethereal style, completely different from the energetic style of more traditional jazz.

Debussy, Claude-Achille (1862–1918). French composer. He was born at St Germain-en-Laye, not far from Paris, and lived in that city most of his life. Debussy's music owes something in spirit both to the work of the Impressionist painters and to the group of French poets called the Symbolists. His own harmonic style, which he developed slowly and carefully, is one of the most original in music, and his influence on twentieth-century music has been great. His principal works for orchestra are *Prélude à l'après-midi d'un faune* ('Prelude to the Afternoon of a Faun'); *Nocturnes*; *La Mer* ('The Sea'); *Images*, including *Ibéria* ('Spain'); and music for the ballet *Jeux*. He wrote one opera, *Pelléas et Mélisande*. His best-known piano works are the *Suite Bergamasque*, which includes 'Clair de lune' ('Moonlight'); *Estampes* ('Prints'), including 'Jardins sous la pluie' ('Gardens in the Rain'); two sets of *Images*; two more substantial sets of preludes, including 'La Fille aux cheveux de lin' ('The Girl with the Flaxen Hair'), 'La Cathédrale engloutie' ('The Sunken Cathedral') and 'Feux d'artifice' ('Fireworks'); the suite *Children's Corner*, including 'Golliwog's Cakewalk'; and twelve studies (*études*). He also composed some important groups of *chansons* (songs), and some instrumental works, including a string quartet.

Above: Claude-Achille Debussy

Right: A very late portrait of Frederick Delius. Blind and paralysed, he dictated his last compositions to Eric Fenby, a younger English composer.

Delibes, Léo (1836–91).
French composer of operas and songs, but best known today for his tuneful and brightly orchestrated music to the ballets *Coppélia* and *Sylvia*.

Delius, Frederick (1862–1934).
English composer, although his family was of German descent and he spent most of his life abroad. He developed a style which owed something to Grieg but was unmistakably his own—noted for its 'fluid' and shifting harmonies. His best-known works are the descriptive orchestral pieces *On Hearing the First Cuckoo in Spring, Summer Night on the River, The Walk to the Paradise Garden* (from the opera *A Village Romeo and Juliet*), and the 'English Rhapsody' *Brigg Fair* (a set of variations on a Lincolnshire folk song). But Delius also wrote some large choral and orchestral works, notably *A Mass of Life* (based on the writings of the German philosopher Nietzsche), which express his strong mystical feelings about Nature.

Donizetti, Gaetano (1797–1848).
Italian composer of operas in the *bel canto* style, both serious (*Lucia di Lammermoor*, based on a novel by Sir Walter Scott) and comic (*Don Pasquale* and *La Fille du régiment*, composed for the Paris Opera).

Dowland, John (1563–1626).
English lutenist and composer who served the king of Denmark for some years, and latterly Charles I of England. His ayres and many compositions or arrangements for the lute are both beautifully expressive and landmarks in the history of song and of instrumental music.

Dufay, Gillaume (about 1400–74).
Netherlands composer who served both the Pope and the Burgundian court during his long and illustrious life. He wrote church masses and secular *chansons* (songs), and among his pupils was the great Jean de Ockeghem.

Dukas, Paul (1865–1935).
French composer and scholar of old music. His own works, influenced by the musical 'impressionism' of Debussy, Ravel and other contemporary figures, include the well-known *L'Apprenti Sorcier* ('The Sorcerer's Apprentice'), an orchestral piece describing how the apprentice dabbles in his master's magic with disastrous results, but the sorcerer returns home in time to save the day.

Dunstable, John
(about 1390–1453).
English composer, mathematician and astrologer who for many years served the Duke of Bedford, Regent of France and brother of Henry V of England. His songs, church masses and motets were greatly admired throughout Western Europe during his lifetime and influenced the music of Binchois, Dufay and others who worked at the court of Burgundy.

Duparc, Henri (1848–1933).
French composer whose output was very small due to a severe mental breakdown. However, he is remembered for a small and very fine group of *chansons* (songs).

Gaetano Donizetti

Antonin Dvořák

Sir Edward Elgar

Dvořák, Antonin (1841–1904). Bohemian-born composer who, with Smetana, worked for Czech national independence; and from humble beginnings became one of the most famous men of his time, crowning his career with an extended visit to the United States. He wrote in almost every musical form of the period, combining something of the style of Brahms (who was his friend) with elements of Bohemian folk song and dance. His works include: nine symphonies—no 9 in E minor, subtitled 'From the New World', being partly inspired by Negro folk songs; the Cello Concerto in B minor; the opera *Rusalka* (named after a water spirit from Slavonic legend); symphonic poems; string quartets and other chamber music compositions; and the popular Slavonic Dances and Slavonic Rhapsodies.

Elgar, Sir Edward (1857–1934). English composer, born near Worcester, who is generally regarded as the greatest since Purcell, and the one who opened the way for other English composers of this century. The work that first won him recognition after years of neglect was the 'Enigma' Variations (full title— Variations on an Original Theme for Orchestra—each variation being a musical portrait of one of his friends). Other important compositions, often written in a rich and vivid style, are: the oratorio *The Dream of Gerontius*; two symphonies; a violin and a cello concerto; the 'symphonic study' *Falstaff* (after the Shakespearian character); and the concert overture *Cockaigne* (an evocation of the spirit of Edwardian London). The main theme from one of his 'Pomp and Circumstance' marches was made into the patriotic hymn 'Land of Hope and Glory', which Elgar came to detest.

Manuel de Falla

Gabriel Fauré

Ellington, Edward Kennedy 'Duke' (1899–1974).
American jazz musician and band leader. 'Duke' Ellington was a major figure in the world of jazz for nearly fifty years, employing some of the other most talented jazz musicians of his time and featuring arrangements and compositions noted for their subtle harmonies and instrumental 'colouring'. Pieces specially associated with him are 'Take the A Train', 'Satin Doll' and 'Cotton Tail'. A later record album, *Such Sweet Thunder*, was inspired by characters from Shakespeare.

Falla, Manuel de (1876–1946).
Spanish pianist and composer. He was born in the southern province of Andalusia, home of flamenco singing and dancing, and the melodies and rhythms of this music run through nearly everything he wrote. This strong feature of his music, and its popular appeal, made him the leading member of the Spanish nationalist group of composers. His principal works are: the opera *La vida breve* ('Life is Short'); the ballets *El amor brujo* ('Love, the Magician', which includes the 'Ritual Fire Dance') and *The Three-Cornered Hat*; *Nights in the Gardens of Spain* for piano and orchestra; and Seven Popular Spanish Songs for soprano. Another unusual but beautiful piece is *Master Peter's Puppet Show*, a kind of miniature opera using marionettes.

Fauré, Gabriel (1845–1924).
French composer, organist and teacher. His refined style and often subtle harmonies influenced his younger French contemporaries, including Ravel. His most significant compositions were his groups of *chansons* (songs), but he also wrote a beautiful setting of the Requiem Mass, incidental music to Maeterlinck's play *Pelléas et Mélisande* (which Debussy turned into an opera), and many chamber-music works and piano pieces. His Pavane for orchestra and chorus is a very popular concert piece.

Field, John (1782–1837).
Irish pianist and composer. He worked with Clementi in his piano-manufacturing business, then settled in St Petersburg (now Leningrad), winning great fame as a pianist on concert tours. He wrote piano concertos and a number of shorter piano pieces called nocturnes which served as a model for Chopin.

Flagstad, Kirsten Marie (1895–1962).
Norwegian operatic soprano, famous for her Wagnerian roles and above all for her singing of Brünnhilde in *Der Ring des Nibelungen*.

Foster, Stephen Collins (1826–64).
American composer of such famous 'drawing-room' ballads as 'Jeannie with the Light Brown Hair', and songs like 'My Old Kentucky Home' and 'Camptown Races' which were tremendously popular around the turn of the century with 'nigger' minstrel shows (supposed to be a style of black man's entertainment).

137

César Franck

Wilhelm Furtwängler

George Gershwin

Franck, César (1822–90).
Belgian composer. In his own
lifetime he was famous as an organist
in Paris, contributing much to the
great tradition of French organ
music; also a much-loved teacher at
the Paris Conservatory. Today he is
best known for his Symphony in D
minor and Symphonic Variations for
piano and orchestra, written in a rich
harmonic style noted for its
'chromaticism'.

**Frederick II ('The Great') of
Prussia** (1712–86).
He was a great patron of music.
J.S.Bach's *Musical Offering* was
written for him, and he also
employed Bach's son Carl Philipp
Emanuel. He was himself a keen
flautist and composed much music
for the flute.

Frescobaldi, Girolamo
(1583–1643).
Italian composer and in his own time
a very famous organist, whose many
compositions for organ and
harpsichord—toccatas and fugues—

had a big influence on the music of
others, especially in Germany.

Furtwängler, Wilhelm
(1886–1954).
German conductor associated chiefly
with the Berlin and Vienna
Philharmonic orchestras and
remembered for the power and
intensity of his interpretations of
Beethoven, Wagner and Bruckner.

Gabrieli, Andrea (about 1510–86).
and his nephew **Giovanni**
(1557–1612).
Italian composers, both organists at St
Mark's Basilica, Venice, who created
a very dramatic 'antiphonal' style of
church music for groups of voices
and instrumentalists, very similar in
effect to modern stereophonic
reproduction. Such grand and
dramatic music also symbolized the
wealth and power of Venice in
Renaissance times.

Geminiani, Francesco
(1687–1762).
Italian violinist and composer. He

was a pupil of Corelli and another big
figure in the development of the
concerto grosso for the violin family
of instruments. He also wrote an
important treatise on the violin.

Gershwin, George (1898–1937).
American song-writer and composer,
of Russian immigrant parents (born
Jacob Gershovitz). Starting his career
in Tin Pan Alley, traditional music-
publishing quarter of New York
City, he went on to write (often to
his brother Ira's lyrics) some of the
most famous songs of the 1920s and
1930s—'Fascinating Rhythm', 'The
Man I Love', 'Our Love is Here to
Stay'. Then for band leader Paul
Whiteman he composed the
Rhapsody in Blue for piano and
orchestra, combining jazz and Latin
American features with more
'symphonic' forms. Later works in
this style are the Piano Concerto in F,
the symphonic poem *An American in
Paris* and the all-Negro opera *Porgy
and Bess* (containing some of his finest
songs—'Summertime', 'Bess, you is
my woman now').

Gesualdo, Carlo
(about 1560–1615).
Italian prince, lutenist and composer of some madrigals noted for their expressive and adventurous harmonies. He is also remembered as the murderer of his wife and her lover.

Gibbons, Orlando (1583–1625).
English organist, virginalist and composer of church music and some very expressive madrigals (including 'The Silver Swan').He also contributed some keyboard pieces to a famous early printed edition called *Parthenia*.

Gieseking, Walter (1895–1956).
German pianist who specialized in French music, notably that of Debussy.

Gigli, Beniamino (1890–1957).
Italian operatic tenor, internationally famous especially for his singing of Verdi and Puccini.

Glazunov, Alexander
(1865–1936).
Russian composer of symphonies, concertos, ballets (including *The Seasons*) and piano music in a conservative, Romantic style and less nationalistic in character than the music of most of his Russian colleagues.

Glinka, Mikhail Ivanovich
(1804–57).
He is often called the 'father of Russian music', since he was the first Russian composer to become widely known both at home and abroad; and his example was a tremendous encouragement to later Russian nationalist composers. Glinka's best-known works are the operas *Ivan Susanin* (originally produced as *A Life for the Tsar*) and *Ruslan and Ludmilla* (the overture to which is a concert favourite).

Gluck, Christoph Willibald
(1714–87).
German composer who visited London and worked mainly in Paris and Vienna. He was a great reforming figure in the history of opera, arguing that music in opera should serve the dramatic action and not ruin it for the sake of convention or the reputation of star singers. These ideas were taken up in different ways by Mozart, Beethoven, Wagner and others. His own operas, mostly based on plays or stories from Classical antiquity, include *Orfeo ed Euridice*, *Alceste* (to which he wrote a famous preface presenting his ideas), *Iphigénie en Tauride* and *Armide*. He also wrote some instrumental music.

Mikhail Glinka

Benny Goodman

Charles Gounod when aged twenty-one.

Goodman, Benny (born 1909).
American jazz clarinettist and band leader who formed some of the most exciting jazz-swing bands of the 1930s and 1940s and was known as the 'King of Swing'. As a highly gifted soloist he also played the clarinet music of Mozart and Weber and commissioned pieces from Hindemith, Bartók and Copland.

Gounod, Charles (1818–93).
French composer of symphonies, oratorios, much church music and, above all, operas, who was also one of the most successful and famous musicians of his age. The ballet music from his opera *Faust* is still widely known, and sometimes the opera itself is still produced, but most of his other music has now gone out of fashion.

Grainger, Percy Aldridge (1882–1961).
Australian-born pianist and composer who lived in England for some years before settling in the United States and becoming an American citizen. He collected and edited British folk music, making a special arrangement of the traditional Irish tune known as the 'Londonderry Air'. His own compositions, light and breezy in style, include *Country Gardens* and *Handel in the Strand*.

Granados, Enrique (1867–1916).
Spanish pianist and composer, and important member of the Spanish nationalist group of composers. His set of piano pieces called *Goyescas* were inspired by the paintings of his fellow-countryman Francisco Goya, and contain the well-known *The Maiden and the Nightingale*. These *Goyescas* also formed the basis of an opera. Granados was a tragic victim of war, when the ship on which he was returning from America was torpedoed and sunk.

Grieg, Edvard Hagerup (1843–1907).
Norwegian composer who developed a distinctive nationalist style based on the folk songs and dances of his native land, and was much honoured both at home and abroad. He is sometimes called a 'miniaturist' because apart from his very popular Piano Concerto in A minor he wrote no large-scale orchestral or choral works and no operas. But his compositions, including the extensive incidental music he wrote for Ibsen's play *Peer Gynt* and the *Holberg Suite*, are always most skilfully constructed and harmonized.

Guido d'Arezzo (about 995–1050).
Italian monk and important figure in the development of musical notation and theory. He is chiefly remembered as the originator of a method of learning music on which the modern Tonic Sol-Fa system is based. He also devised a method of teaching music to choirs called the 'Guidonian Hand', using sections of the fingers to represent different notes.

Handel, George Frideric (1685–1759).
German-born composer (originally named Georg Friedrich Händel) who settled in London and became a British subject. His life fluctuated between periods of great success and others of failure and hardship, largely because he chose to run his own affairs rather than seek the patronage of church or state. At first he devoted his time largely to opera, composing in rapid succession a number of such works in the fashionable Italian *opera seria* style. Among these are *Rinaldo*, *Berenice* (still famous for its overture), *Julius Caesar*, *Orlando* and *Xerxes* (from which comes the aria known as 'Handel's Largo'). When this type of opera went out of fashion, and after recovery from illness, Handel turned his attention more to oratorio, composing such works as *Saul*, *Israel in Egypt*, *Judas Maccabeus*, *Solomon*

(including 'Arrival of the Queen of Sheba') and, above all, *Messiah* (containing the 'Hallelujah Chorus'). Handel also wrote much instrumental music, including *Music for the Royal Fireworks* and the *Water Music*, pieces in the concerto grosso form, organ concertos (originally often played by Handel himself during the intervals of oratorio performances), sonatas for various instruments, and the well-known set of harpsichord variations nicknamed, but not by the composer, 'The Harmonious Blacksmith'. Handel's robust style of Baroque music has remained very popular in English-speaking countries. It has also been much admired by other great composers. Beethoven said, 'When Handel chooses, he can strike like a thunderbolt!'

Harris, Roy Ellsworth (born 1898).
Eminent American composer and teacher. He has made use of American folk song and dance, but re-creating it in an up-to-date style that gives much of his music a strong spacious sound. His compositions include symphonies, concertos and chamber music.

Haydn, Franz Joseph (1732–1809).
Austrian composer of humble peasant origins who became musical director for many years at the court of the Esterházy family, and as a famous man made two highly successful visits to London. Haydn perfected the Classical forms of the symphony, string quartet and keyboard sonata, thus laying the foundations for Beethoven, Brahms and other great symphonic composers who followed him. He is officially credited with 104 symphonies, of which the last twelve were specially written for London and are known collectively as the 'Salomon Symphonies' after the violinist Johann Peter Salomon, who organized the composer's visits. Many of the symphonies have nicknames, with or without some reason, such as 'Farewell', 'Bear',

'Surprise', 'Clock', 'Miracle', 'Drumroll', 'Military'. Of his eighty string quartets, the so-called 'Emperor' Quartet is the most famous because it contains the melody which later became the national anthem first of the Austrian Empire and today of the German Federal Republic. Haydn also wrote operas and masses, mostly for the court at Esterházy, and towards the end of his life two oratorios, *The Creation* and *The Seasons*. His brother Michael (1737–1806) was *Kapellmeister* to the Archbishop of Salzburg and a composer mainly of church music.

Heifetz, Jascha (born 1901).
Russian-born violinist who settled in the United States and adopted American nationality. He won international fame and commissioned concertos from several composers, including Walton.

Henze, Hans Werner (born 1926).
German composer who has used twelve-tone methods of composition, and also written some music for jazz band and symphony orchestra. Several of his stage works have made a big impression, including the opera *Elegy for Young Lovers* (based on an English libretto by W.H. Auden) and the dramatic oratorio *The Raft of the Medusa*, inspired by Géricault's famous painting, and dedicated to the revolutionary leader Che Guevara.

Herman, Woodrow Wilson, 'Woody' (born 1913).
American jazz clarinettist and leader of a series of famous jazz-swing bands usually called the 'Herman Herd'. His own playing inspired Stravinsky to write his 'Ebony' Concerto ('ebony stick' being a slang name for a clarinet).

Hindemith, Paul (1895–1963).
German violinist, viola-player and composer who eventually settled in the United States after the Nazis came to power. He composed a good

deal of what is called *Gebrauchsmusik* ('Utility Music'), meaning music intended to be an everyday part of people's lives rather than more elevated 'art' music. Two of his other works remain popular in the concert hall: the symphony *Mathis der Maler* (based on music taken from his opera about the German Renaissance painter Mathäus Grünewald), and the *Symphonic Metamorphoses on Themes of Weber*, the rather severe title for some very entertaining music.

Holiday, Billie (1915–59).
Jazz vocalist recognized as one of the greatest interpreters of Blues and Blues-style music. For about twenty years she sang with many of the finest jazz instrumentalists, but as with many other talented and sensitive jazz musicians the pressures of her way of life destroyed her career and led to her premature death.

Holst, Gustav (1874–1934).
English composer of Swedish descent, also a noted teacher. His orchestral suite *The Planets*—in which the astrological character of each of the individual planets is portrayed in turn—combines his inspired orchestration and highly distinctive harmonic style with his deep interest in mysticism. Other works are the equally mystical *Hymn of Jesus* for chorus and orchestra, the opera *The Perfect Fool*, and the symphonic poem *Egdon Heath*.

Honegger, Arthur (1892–1955).
Swiss composer, but born in France and one of the French group of composers known as 'Les Six'. Like the others of this group, he soon branched out creatively on his own, his works including the oratorio *King David* and music to the play *Joan of Arc at the Stake*. Another piece, at one time very well known, was his orchestral *Pacific 231*, conveying the sound and motion of a steam railway locomotive.

Gustav Holst

Leoš Janáček

Horowitz, Vladimir (born 1904).
Russian-born pianist who settled in
the United States and earned the
highest reputation for his dazzling
technique. Illness terminated his
concert career in 1950. He is married
to Toscanini's daughter Wanda.

Hovhaness, Alan (born 1911).
American conductor, organist and
composer. His family were
Armenian, and his own compositions
have been much influenced by Asiatic
and Middle Eastern music. One of
these is the concerto for piano and
strings with the Armenian title
Lousadzak ('The Coming of Light').
Another interesting work is *And God
Created Great Whales*, which uses the
recorded sounds of a whale.

Hummel, Johann Nepomuk
(1778–1837).
Austrian pianist and composer, a
pupil of Haydn, Mozart and
Clementi, very famous in his own
day as a performer, and composer of
piano concertos and other piano
works in an attractive blend of
Classical and early Romantic styles.

Humperdinck, Engelbert
(1854–1921).
German composer, a close friend and
colleague of Wagner, now chiefly
remembered for his opera *Hansel and
Gretel* (based on the one of the fairy
tales of the brothers Grimm).

Ibert, Jacques (1890–1962).
French composer, not a member of
'Les Six', but writing music in the
same light, sometimes irreverent
style. His works include the
orchestral *Escales* ('Ports of Call') and
Divertissement, and piano pieces such
as 'Le petit âne blanc' ('The Little
White Donkey').

Ireland, John (1879–1962).
English composer whose music is
generally written in a Romantic but
quite personal style. His works
include a piano concerto, the *London*
concert overture and his well-known
setting of John Masefield's poem 'Sea
Fever'.

Ives, Charles (1874–1954).
American composer who combined
writing music with a successful
business career. In fact, he was an
astonishingly advanced and original
musical thinker, though having very
little contact with other more
established composers of his time,
such as Schoenberg and Bartók. His
compositions, mostly inspired by
places and events in his home
territory of New England, include
the orchestral *Three Places in New
England* and the 'Concord' Piano
Sonata.

Janáček, Leoš (1854–1928).
Czech composer whose music is both
strongly nationalistic in character and
original in style, being based largely
on the sound of the Czech language.
This is particularly the case with his
operas, *Jenůfa*, *Katya Kabanova*, *The
Cunning Little Vixen* (which also
reflects many sounds from nature),
The Makropoulos Affair and *From the
House of the Dead*. Other works
include the *Glagolitic Mass* for chorus
and orchestra (Glagolitic being an old
Slav church language), the orchestral
Sinfonietta, the symphonic poem
Taras Bulba, and the String Quartet
called *Intimate Letters*.

Joachim, Joseph (1831–1907).
Hungarian violinist and close friend
of Brahms who often consulted him
on technical matters and whose
Violin Concerto is dedicated to him.
However, Joachim was also a
composer in his own right, his works
including three violin concertos and
concert overtures.

Joplin, Scott (1868–1917).
American jazz pianist and composer.
The son of an ex-slave, Scott Joplin
hoped to transform ragtime and
other early jazz styles into concert
music, and when he failed to do this
sank into deep depression. Today he
is remembered for such charming
piano pieces as 'Maple Leaf Rag' and
'The Entertainer'. He also wrote an
opera.

Josquin des Prés
(about 1450–1521).
Netherlands composer who served
the Pope for some years and then the
French court. He was much revered
in his own time, notably by Luther.
Today we recognize him as one of
the key figures of Renaissance music,
bringing a new freshness and vigour
to choral music of all kinds in a style
known as *musica reservata*—a Latin
term probably meaning music
reserved for those with finer feelings.

Karajan, Herbert von (born 1908).
Austrian conductor closely associated
with the Berlin Philharmonic
Orchestra, the Vienna State Opera
and the Salzburg Easter Festival. He is
noted above all for the refined sound
and precision of his performances.

Kern, Jerome (1885–1945).
American song-writer who did most
to transform the European style of
operetta into the American stage and
film musical, his most celebrated
achievement in this field being *Show
Boat*. He also composed some works
for orchestra, including *Portrait of
Mark Twain*.

Zoltán Kodály

Khachaturian, Aram (1903–78).
Soviet Armenian composer who
made use of the folk music of his
homeland in many of his own works.
Among these is the ballet *Gayaneh*
containing the famous 'Sabre Dance'.

Kodály, Zoltán (1882–1967).
Hungarian composer who for some
time worked with his compatriot
Bartók in the field of folk music. This
shared interest has given their music
some points in common, although
Kodály soon developed his own
distinctive musical personality. His
compositions include the strongly
nationalistic *Psalmus Hungaricus* for
chorus and orchestra, the orchestral
Dances from Galanta and the
orchestral suite from his opera *Háry
János* which opens with a famous
musical 'sneeze', an indication,
according to Hungarian custom, that
the adventures of the folk hero Háry
János should not be taken too
seriously!

Korngold, Erich Wolfgang
(1897–1957).
Austrian-born composer who settled
in the United States and became an
American citizen. His works include
operas and concertos, but during the
1930s he moved to Hollywood and
specialized in writing film music.

Kreisler, Fritz (1875–1926).
Austrian violinist acclaimed for the
lyrical style of his playing. He also
composed some music, including a
number of violin pieces which he at
first credited to other dead composers,
including Gaetano Pugnani,
but then admitted to be his own.

Landino, Francesco
(about 1325–97).
Italian lutenist and composer, an
important representative of the *ars
nova* school of music and composer of
secular part-songs which led directly
to the development of the madrigal.
He was blind from childhood.

Lassus, Orlandus (1530–94).
Netherlands composer and one of the
most important figures of
Renaissance music. He was in great
demand as a choirmaster and director
of music, holding posts in Rome and
Antwerp and at the Bavarian court in
Munich, where he died. Lassus
composed more than 2000 choral and
vocal works—church masses and
motets, also many secular madrigals
—in the finest polyphonic style. He
is sometimes called by the Italian version of his name—Orlando di Lasso.

Lehár, Franz (1870–1948).
Hungarian composer of many
successful Viennese-style operettas,
notably *The Merry Widow*.

Leoncavallo, Ruggiero
(1858–1919).
Italian operatic composer. One of his
operas was a version of *La Bohème*,
but his only real success was *I
Pagliacci* ('The Clowns'), a story of
real-life drama among a group of
travelling players.

Léonin (about 1130–80).
French choirmaster of the so-called
Notre Dame School of Paris, and one
of the earliest people in Western
music to be known by name as a
composer. He compiled a *Great Book
of Organum* containing music for all
the main events of the church year.
Also sometimes known by the Latin
version of his name—Leoninus.

Lind, Jenny (1820–87).
Swedish soprano who attracted huge
audiences both in the United States
and in Britain and was one of the
highest-paid of all concert artists. She
was known as 'The Swedish
Nightingale'.

Liszt, Franz (or Ferencz)
(1811–86).
Hungarian pianist and composer.
Liszt was a major figure in
nineteenth-century music, first as a
tremendously successful concert
pianist, then, as musical director to

Franz Liszt

the court of Weimar, a serious composer, teacher and friend of many of
the other great musical figures of his
time. After a socially unconventional
life, including several famous love
affairs, he finally took holy orders in
the Roman Catholic Church, becoming known as the 'Abbé Liszt'.
He also held strong nationalist
feelings and at the end of his life
presided over the newly founded
Hungarian Academy of Music in
Budapest. As a composer Liszt made
important contributions to the field
of Romantic programme music. For
the orchestra he wrote the 'Faust'
Symphony (with a choral ending),
and in a number of other descriptive
orchestral works created the form of
the symphonic poem. For the piano
he composed some equally vivid
descriptive pieces, notably those
included in his albums called *Années
de Pèlerinage* ('Years of Pilgrimage').
In his Piano Sonata in B minor he
also introduced important new ideas
in musical structure and form; while
his Hungarian Rhapsodies and some
of his piano transcriptions of themes
from operas reflect his own
phenomenal pianistic technique. His
very popular 'Liebestraum' ('Dream
of Love') is a piano transcription of
one of his own songs.

Lully, Jean-Baptiste (1632–87). French composer—actually born in Italy as Giovanni Battista Lulli—who rose to a position of great power and importance at the court of Louis XIV at Versailles. He created a brilliant new form of opera-ballet, and in his overtures to these works influenced the development of Baroque orchestral music. Lully also collaborated with some of the other famous Frenchmen of his time, including Molière. His end was most unfortunate: he accidentally banged his foot with his heavy conducting staff and died of blood poisoning.

Luther, Martin (1483–1546). German priest and monk and leader of the Protestant Reformation, but also a gifted musician. He introduced a new form of church hymn called the chorale. 'Ein feste Burg' ('A Safe Stronghold is our God') is the best-known of these, sometimes called the Battle Hymn of the Reformation. Later composers, including J.S. Bach, quoted from these chorales.

Macdowell, Edward (1861–1908). American pianist and composer who studied and then taught in Europe for some years before returning to the United States. He won much popularity in his own lifetime, on both sides of the Atlantic, on account of his piano concertos and many other shorter piano pieces, written in an attractive Lisztian style. After his death the Macdowell Colony in New England was founded as a retreat for other composers, writers and artists.

Machaut, Guillaume de (about 1300–77). French priest, poet and composer. He was a leading member of the *ars nova* school or style of music with his settings of both religious and secular texts, often composed in a very elaborate polyphonic style. Among his works is one of the earliest surviving complete settings of the church mass.

Gustav Mahler

Mahler, Gustav (1860–1911). Austrian conductor and composer. As a conductor, mainly of opera in Vienna and New York, Mahler demanded and obtained the highest standards of performance. As a composer he sometimes used his music to convey his own inner conflicts and anxieties, sometimes to express great philosophical or religious themes; while at the same time he pointed the way to technical advances in twentieth-century music through his harmonies and orchestration. His principal works are nine completed symphonies (plus a tenth recently completed from his notes), all written for a very large orchestra and generally long and complex in construction. Nos 2 ('Resurrection'), 3, 4 and 8 (the 'Symphony of a Thousand') also require vocal soloists, a chorus, or both. In addition, Mahler composed several orchestral song-cycles, including *Kindertotenlieder* ('Songs on the Death of Children') and *Das Lied von der Erde* ('The Song of the Earth').

Dame Nellie Melba

Melba, Nellie (1861–1931).
Australian operatic soprano. She took
her professional name from her
birthplace—Melbourne—and was
one of the most fêted singers of her
age. Like Caruso, she added greatly
to her fame and reputation as one of
the earliest serious recording artists.

Mendelssohn-Bartholdy, Felix
(1809–47).
German conductor and composer,
usually just called Mendelssohn. He
was tremendously popular and
successful during his own lifetime
and for many years afterwards,
combining in his music Romantic
feeling with a restrained and Classical
sense of form. His best-known works
are: the truly magical overture to
Shakespeare's *A Midsummer Night's
Dream* (composed at the age of
seventeen), with other incidental
music to the play, including the
famous 'Wedding March', written
later; five symphonies—no 3 (the
'Scottish'), no 4 (the 'Italian'), no 5
(the 'Reformation'); the well-loved
Violin Concerto in E minor; the
concert overture *The Hebrides* (or
'Fingal's Cave', inspired by a visit to
the Western Isles of Scotland); much
chamber music, and several albums of
piano pieces called *Lieder ohne Worte*
('Songs Without Words', which
include such pieces as the so-called
'Bees' Wedding' and 'Spring Song').
As a conductor Mendelssohn was in
great demand both in Germany and
in Britain. It was specially for English
audiences, with their love of
Handelian oratorio, that he
composed his own oratorio *Elijah*.

Menotti, Gian-Carlo (born 1911).
Italian-born composer who has lived
and worked in the United States for
most of his life. His best-known
works are a series of operas, generally
written in a clear tuneful style and
some originally intended for tele-
vision, including *Amelia Goes to the
Ball*, *The Medium*, *The Telephone*,
Amahl and the Night Visitors and *The
Saint of Bleecker Street*.

Martinů, Bohuslav (1890–1959).
Czech composer who lived in France
for some years and then settled in the
United States. He wrote operas,
symphonies, symphonic poems and
much instrumental music in a highly
personal but less nationalistic style
than that adopted by Smetana,
Dvořák, Janáček and other Czech
composers before him.

Mascagni, Pietro (1863–1945).
Italian operatic composer who, like
his near contemporary and fellow
countryman Leoncavallo, had just
one big success. This was *Cavalleria
Rusticana* ('Rustic Chivalry'), a
drama of Sicilian revenge and murder
in the realistic style of *verismo* opera.

Massenet, Jules (1842–1912).
French composer, mainly of operas
written in a clear, lyrical style.
Manon, based on the novel *Manon
Lescaut* by the Abbé Prévost which
Puccini also used, is Massenet's best-
known opera today. He also wrote
many songs.

Yehudi Menuhin

Menuhin, Yehudi (born 1916).
American violinist whose boyhood
fame included a remarkable association with Elgar, with whom he made
some recordings. During his
distinguished career Menuhin has
commissioned works from such
composers as Bartók, and helped to
foster international goodwill with his
work among young musicians of all
nationalities. He also sometimes
conducts.

Messiaen, Olivier (born 1908).
French composer whose most
original style—almost a new musical
'language'—has been formed by his
varied interests in such matters as
religion and mysticism, the harmonic
and rhythmic features of Indian
music, and bird-song. He has written
much organ music, notably
L'Ascension and *La Nativité du
Seigneur* ('The Birth of Our Lord');
piano works, including his *Catalogue
d'Oiseaux* ('Catalogue of Birds'); and
orchestral compositions, often with
very exotic percussion effects,
including the massive 'Turangalîla'
Symphony (which also has a part for
the electronic *Ondes Martenot*).

Meyerbeer, Jakob (or Giacomo)
(1791–1864).
German composer who worked
mainly in Paris, composing a series of
operas, very popular in their day,
noted for their spectacular themes
and grandiose musical style. The
most famous of them, *Les Huguenots*,
deals with the massacre of French
Protestant Huguenots.

Milhaud, Darius (1892–1974).
French composer and originally a
member of the group of composers
known as 'Les Six'. His output was
considerable, much of it influenced
by his interest in Latin American
music and jazz. One of his best-
known works of this kind is the ballet
La Création du monde ('The Creation
of the World').

Miller, Glenn (1904–44).
American dance band leader,
immensely popular during the 1930s
and 1940s on account of such famous
swing numbers as 'In the Mood',
'Moonlight Serenade' and 'A String
of Pearls'. As a US army officer he
came to Britain with his band and
was lost on a flight to France.

Monteverdi, Claudio (1567–1643).
Italian composer who held various
court and church appointments, the
last and most important of these
being as director of music to the
Basilica of St Mark, Venice. He
wrote much fine and dramatic
church music in the antiphonal style
specially associated with St Mark's,
also many madrigals, including some
madrigali spirituali to religious words.
Above all, Monteverdi is
remembered as the first great
composer of opera and also, because
of his imaginative use of instruments
in his operas, as a pioneer figure in the
history of the orchestra. Many of his
operas have been lost. Three that
survive are *Orfeo*, *Il Ritorno
d'Ulisse in Patria* ('The Return
of Ulysses') and *L'Incoronazione di
Poppea* ('The Coronation of Poppea',
being based on events in the life
of the Emperor Nero).

Morley, Thomas (1557–1603).
English organist and composer. A
pupil of Byrd, Morley wrote music
for the church, to both Latin and
English texts, many instrumental
pieces for the lute, viols and virginal,
and some of the finest madrigals of
the Elizabethan period (contributing
to the famous madrigal collection
called *The Triumphs of Oriana*). He
almost certainly knew Shakespeare
and composed songs for some of his
plays, notably 'It was a Lover and his
Lass' (in *As You Like It*). He also
wrote an entertaining book called
*Plaine and Easie Introduction to
Practicall Musicke*.

Morton, Ferdinand 'Jelly Roll'
(1885–1941).
American jazz pianist whose real
name was Ferdinand Joseph La
Menthe. He recorded some of his best
music with a celebrated group called
the 'Red Hot Peppers'. Years later he
recorded reminiscences of his
colourful life in New Orleans and
examples of early jazz styles specially
for the American Library of
Congress.

Oliver Messiaen

Jakob Meyerbeer

Mozart, Wolfgang Amadeus
(1756–91).
Austrian composer. He was born in
Salzburg and began life as a child
prodigy, being taken round the
courts of Europe by his father and
winning much praise and fame. As a
young man he held a post with the
Archbishop of Salzburg, but when
this ended he was largely thrown
back on his own resources. He was in
demand as a performer and composer
and achieved great success with some
of his operas, but did not have the
temperament to manage his affairs or
make his own way in the world and
died in poverty, in Vienna. Much of
Mozart's music is written in the
charming eighteenth-century
Rococo style, intended as social
entertainment. His greatest music
occurs in his operas or in those
orchestral and instrumental works
which combine mastery of Classical
form with great expressive power
and sometimes very advanced musical
thinking. Mozart's principal operas
are *Idomeneo*, *Die Entführung aus
dem Serail* ('The Escape from the
Harem', also known as *Il Seraglio*), *Le
Nozze di Figaro* ('The Marriage of
Figaro'), *Don Giovanni*, *Così fan tutte*
(loosely translated as 'Women are all
the same'), *Die Zauberflöte* ('The
Magic Flute') and *La Clemenza di
Tito* ('The Mercy of Titus'). His
greatest orchestral and instrumental
works include the symphonies no 36
in C major ('Linz' K425,), no 38 in D
major ('Prague', K504), no 39 in E
flat major (K543), no 40 in G minor
(K550), and the last, no 41 in C major
('Jupiter', K551); the piano concertos
in D minor (K466), in C minor
(K491), and in C major (K503); the
string quintets in C major (K515), in
G minor (K516) and in D major
(K593); and the six string quartets he
dedicated to Haydn, including those
in G major (K387), in D minor
(K421), and in C major ('Dissonance',
K465). His last commission was for a
setting of the Requiem Mass (K626),
which he morbidly believed he was
writing for himself. In fact, he did die

Wolfgang Amadeus Mozart

before finishing the work, completed
later by a pupil. Today Mozart's
compositions are usually quoted with
their 'K' number, after the scholar
Ludwig von Köchel who catalogued
and indexed them in their probable
chronological order.

Mussorgsky, Modest (1839–81).
Russian composer and perhaps the
most naturally gifted member of the
group of nationalist composers
known as 'The Five'. Mussorgsky
was an army officer and later a civil
servant; consequently his output of
music was small, but of great
originality. He composed some
remarkable songs which share with
Janáček's music a deep feeling for the
rhythms and inflections of speech; the
equally remarkable piano work
Pictures at an Exhibition (prompted by
a memorial exhibition of the work of
an artist friend and later vividly
orchestrated by Ravel); the
symphonic poem *Night on the Bare
Mountain*; and the opera *Boris
Godunov*, based on events in Russian
history. He died from drink leaving
several other works unfinished.

Nicolai, Otto (1810–49).
German conductor, and composer of the opera *The Merry Wives of Windsor* (after the play by Shakespeare). He also has a place in musical history as founder-conductor of the world-famous Vienna Philharmonic Orchestra.

Nielsen, Carl (1865–1931).
Danish composer, generally regarded as his country's greatest. Like his exact contemporary Sibelius in Finland, Nielsen reacted against the weighty, emotional character of late Romantic and post-Wagnerian music with a series of symphonies which are, by comparison, fresh and direct in content and form. Of his six symphonies, no 2 is called 'The Four Temperaments' (its movements being based on the old idea of the four aspects of human personality—choleric, phlegmatic, melancholic, sanguine), no 3 is *Sinfonia Espansiva*, and no 4 is the 'Unquenchable' (sometimes translated as 'Inextinguishable'). He also wrote operas, orchestral concertos for various instruments, concert overtures, and chamber music.

Obrecht, Jacob (about 1451–1505).
Netherlands composer, noted for his use of melodies from secular *chansons* and folk songs in his church masses and motets, and for the comparatively warm and spontaneous character of much of his music.

Ockeghem, Jean de
(about 1425–95).
Netherlands composer, in service to the French court for many years. He was also a great and influential teacher, known among his contemporaries as 'The Prince of Music'. Ockeghem's elaborate polyphonic style, in which the individual melodic lines, or parts, often follow one another in an 'imitative' way, helped to prepare the way for the fugues and similar contrapuntal works of Bach, over two hundred years later. He also wrote secular French *chansons*.

Jacques Offenbach

Ignacy Paderewski

Offenbach, Jacques (1819–80).
German born but by adoption a French composer, achieving tremendous success with a series of nearly ninety tuneful and light-hearted operettas. The best known of these today are *La Belle Hélène* and *Orpheus in the Underworld* (containing the famous can-can). His opera *The Tales of Hoffmann* (based on the work of the German writer E.T.A. Hoffmann) is more serious in character.

Oliver, Joseph 'King' (1885–1938).
American cornet player and band leader, and one of the pioneers of jazz. He led a band in the Storeyville district of New Orleans between 1910 and 1917, then moved to Chicago, forming his famous Creole Jazz Band and making some of the finest recordings in the best New Orleans style. Louis Armstrong worked closely with him for some years.

Orff, Carl (born 1895).
German composer and prominent figure in the field of musical education. He composed operas and other stage works; but his best-known work today is the *Carmina Burana*, a type of cantata, setting to music medieval verses mostly to do with drinking and love, and written in a bright and entertaining style.

Ory, Edward 'Kid' (1889–1973).
American jazz trombonist and band leader, working with Joe 'King' Oliver, 'Jelly Roll' Morton, Louis Armstrong, Sidney Bechet and other leading exponents of early jazz. He continued playing, on and off, right up to the 1960s, his composition 'Muskrat Ramble' having become a big hit.

Paderewski, Ignacy (1860–1941).
Polish pianist of immense popularity during the earlier part of this century, also composer. He became the first Prime Minister of the newly founded Polish state in 1919 and later Speaker of the exiled Polish parliament at the outbreak of the Second World War.

Above: Giovanni Pierluigi da Palestrina

Right: Adelina Patti

Paganini, Niccolò (1782–1840).
Italian violinist, and the most celebrated of all virtuoso violin players
on account of his almost freakish
command of the instrument. This,
and his awkward, cadaverous appearance, gave rise to legends associating
him with the Devil—which all
helped to draw the crowds wherever
he went. As a composer Paganini
wrote five violin concertos and a
number of works for solo violin which
reflect his astonishing technique. One
of his capriccios is very well known
because Brahms, Rachmaninov and
others have used it as the basis
for compositions of their own.

Palestrina, Giovanni Pierluigi da
(about 1525–94).
Italian composer (named after his
birthplace near Rome). He spent
most of his life in service to the Pope,
creating a 'pure' polyphonic style in
his masses, motets and other religious
works that has been highly regarded
since. His *Missa Papae Marcelli* ('Mass
for Pope Marcellus') was long believed to have saved music from
being banned in church at the time of
the Roman Catholic Counter-
Reformation, on account of its
heaven-inspired beauty, but there is
probably no historical truth in this.
Palestrina also composed some mad-

rigals, and outside church affairs he
was a successful businessman.

Parker, Charlie 'Bird' (1920–55).
American jazz saxophonist and one of
the most original and daring of jazz
musicians. With trumpeter Dizzy
Gillespie, pianist Thelonius Monk
and a few others, he created the style
known as Bebop, which broke up all
existing jazz conventions and opened
the way for even more radical styles.
Like some of the other most gifted
jazz musicians, Parker could not stand
up to the pressures of his way of life
and died young from drink and
drugs.

Patti, Adelina (1843–1919).
Italian operatic soprano whose parents settled in the United States when she was a child. She achieved fame and fortune, notably for her singing of the *bel canto* roles in Bellini, Donizetti and Rossini, and for her parts in French opera.

Pedrell, Felipe (1841–1922).
Spanish musical historian who edited and revived much old Spanish music. He is also regarded as founder of the Spanish nationalist school, being the teacher of Granados and Falla.

Pergolesi, Giovanni Battista (1710–36).
Italian composer, mainly of operas, whose *La Serva padrona* ('The Maid as Mistress') in the *opera buffa* style caused a big quarrel between the supporters of Italian and French opera—known as the 'War of the Buffoons'—when it was staged in Paris. Stravinsky's ballet *Pulcinella* is loosely based on Pergolesi's music.

Peri, Jacopo (1561–1633).
Italian priest and composer, and member of the group of musicians and other artists known as the *Camerata* ('Fellowship'), whose attempted revival of Classical Greek drama is regarded as the true beginning of opera. In this context, Peri's *Euridice* was one of the first operas to be staged.

Pérotin, or Perotinus Magnus (about 1160–1220).
French choirmaster and composer, and, with his older colleague Léonin, associated with the so-called Notre Dame School of music in Paris. They were both pioneers in early forms of polyphony, their work belonging to what is known as the *ars antiqua*, or Old Art, as distinct from the *ars nova*, or New Art, of their successors.

Porter, Cole (1893–1964).
American song-writer who composed the lyrics—often extremely witty and sophisticated—as well as the melodies to most of his songs. Among his celebrated numbers are 'Let's Do It', 'You're the Top' and 'Night and Day'; his many successful stage and film musicals include *Kiss Me Kate* (based on Shakespeare's *The Taming of the Shrew*), *Can Can* and *High Society*. He was crippled by a riding accident and lived in constant pain for many years after.

Poulenc, Francis (1899–1963).
French pianist and composer, and originally a member of the group called 'Les Six'. He developed a clear and elegant style, but one capable of expressing real feeling. His works include the opera *Les Dialogues des Carmélites* (a story of Carmelite nuns during the French Revolution), the ballet *Les Biches*, several concertos, piano pieces, and many songs.

Praetorius
The Latin name taken by many sixteenth- and seventeenth-century German musicians. Most famous is Michael Praetorius (1571–1621), who composed motets, madrigals and instrumental pieces, and also wrote a book which sums up the musical knowledge and thinking of his time.

Prokofiev, Sergei (1891–1953).
Soviet Russian pianist and composer. He left the Soviet Union soon after the Bolshevik Revolution, composing music noted at the time for its difficulty and dissonance. Returning to his homeland, he modified his style in accordance with Soviet policy, producing music with a much wider appeal. His works include seven symphonies—no 1 is the popular 'Classical' Symphony; several concertos; piano sonatas and other instrumental works; the opera *War and Peace* (based on Tolstoy's novel); the ballets *Cinderella* and *Romeo and Juliet* (after Shakespeare); *Peter and the Wolf* (a Russian folk tale for narrator and orchestra); and music for several films, notably *Lieutenant Kije* and some which were directed by Sergei Eisenstein.

Sergei Prokofiev

Giacomo Puccini with a character from Madame Butterfly

Henry Purcell

Purcell, Henry (1659–95).
English composer, remembered
today especially for his stage works,
including the opera *Dido and Aeneas*
which has some of the most expressive music ever set to English
words; and *The Fairy Queen*, a semi-
operatic version of Shakespeare's *A
Midsummer Night's Dream*. Purcell
also wrote several cantata-like pieces
called odes, intended for special
occasions, and instrumental compositions, including the so-called
'Golden' Sonata. The well-known
'Trumpet Voluntary', long attributed
to him, is now known to be by his
close contemporary Jeremiah Clarke
and was originally called 'The Prince
of Denmark's March'.

Quantz, Johann Joachim
(1697–1773)
German composer, mainly of music
for the flute. He was employed by
Frederick the Great, teaching his
royal master to play the instrument.

Quilter, Roger (1877–1953)
English composer of many attractive
songs and *A Children's Overture*.

Puccini, Giacomo (1858–1924).
Italian composer, almost exclusively
of opera. His output was small compared with that of his great predecessor Verdi, but five of the operas he
did produce are now among the most
popular in the repertory, combining
beautifully constructed melodies
with a clear and vivid orchestration.
They are *Manon Lescaut*, *La Bohème*,
Tosca, *Madame Butterfly* and *Turandot*
(completed by Franco Alfano after
his death). His one-act comedy
Gianni Schicchi (forming part of a
group of three one-act operas called *Il
Trittico*, or 'The Triptych') is also a
great favourite. Another interesting
opera is *La Fanciulla del West* ('The
Girl of the Golden West'), set in
California at the time of the famous
gold-rush. Puccini also contributed
to the operatic style called *verismo*
('realism'), with its emphasis on basic
human emotions or situations.

Sergei Rachmaninov

Maurice Ravel

Rachmaninov, Sergei Vassilievich (1873–1943). Russian pianist and composer. He left Russia soon after the Bolshevik Revolution, finally settling in the United States; but he remained deeply attached in a spiritual sense to his homeland, expressing his feelings in music written in a late Romantic style and characteristically melancholy mood. His principal compositions are: four piano concertos, plus the Rhapsody on a Theme of Paganini; three symphonies; the symphonic poem *The Isle of the Dead* (inspired by a painting of the same name); a cantata *The Bells* (after the poem by Edgar Allen Poe); Symphonic Dances for orchestra; and many pieces for solo piano. As a pianist—possibly the greatest of his generation—Rachmaninov made recordings of his own and other composers' music.

Rameau, Jean Philippe (1683–1764). French organist, harpsichordist and composer. For many years he concentrated, like his older colleague Couperin, on the composition of keyboard music, then produced a series of spectacular and very strikingly written opera-ballets, including *Les Indes Galantes* ('The Courtly Indies'). It was his operas and those of the Italian Pergolesi that produced the musical controversy called 'The War of the Buffoons'. Rameau also wrote several important books on musical theory, which are now interesting for the light they throw on eighteenth-century musical thinking.

Ravel, Maurice (1875–1937). French composer and colleague of Fauré, Debussy, Satie and members of 'Les Six'. His music expresses something of the character of each of these people or groups in turn, while developing along very individual lines of its own. Ravel was a superb orchestrator, his masterpiece in this field being his score to the ballet *Daphnis et Chloé*. Other great examples of his orchestration can be heard in the operas *L'Enfant et les sortilèges* (loosely translated as 'The Spellbound Child', with libretto by Colette) and *L'Heure Espagnole* ('The Spanish Hour'); the orchestral song-cycle *Shéhérazade*; the two jazz-influenced piano concertos (one for the left hand only) and the *Bolero*. His piano music includes the impressionistic *Miroirs* ('Mirrors', including 'Alborada del gracioso'), *Mother Goose* suite and *Gaspard de la Nuit* ('Phantoms of the Night'); also pieces modelled on past styles, *Valses Nobles et Sentimentales* and *Le Tombeau de Couperin* (much of this music being later orchestrated by the composer). Ravel also wrote several notable chamber music and instrumental works—a string quartet, piano trio, Introduction and Allegro for flute, harp and string quartet, and a violin sonata.

Reinhardt, Django (1910–53).
Belgian gipsy guitarist, and the first great European jazz musician. His left hand was severely burned in a caravan fire, which forced him to give up the violin in favour of the guitar, but he teamed up with the violinist Stephane Grappelly, to lead the unique Quintet of the Hot Club de France. This famous group broke up at the start of the Second World War, but Reinhardt continued playing, and just after the war made some appearances with Duke Ellington.

Respighi, Ottorino (1879-1936).
Italian composer of two dazzling orchestral pieces, *The Pines of Rome* and *The Fountains of Rome*, but also of more restrained works such as *Three Botticelli Pictures* and the orchestral suite *The Birds* (based on music of the seventeenth and eighteenth centuries, and reflecting Respighi's scholarly interest in old music). Another of his works is the ballet *La Boutique fantasque* ('The Fantastic Toyshop'), based on music by Rossini.

Riegger, Wallingford
(1885–1961).
American composer. He studied in Germany for some years, developing a style based partly on twelve-tone methods of composition. His works include three symphonies, and much music for the Martha Graham and other dance companies.

Rimsky-Korsakov, Nicolai Andreivich (1844–1908).
Russian composer, and leading member of the nationalist group known as 'The Five'. He started life as a naval officer, and only began to develop his own style of composition after he had been appointed as a professor to the St Petersburg Musical Conservatory. Above all, Rimsky-Korsakov was a gifted and inspired orchestrator, his works including the operas *The Snow Maiden* and *The Golden Cockerel* (a work of political satire that was banned in Russia until after his death), the

Nicolai Rimsky-Korsakov

orchestral suite *Sheherazade* (inspired by *Tales from the Arabian Nights*), the *Capriccio Espagnol* ('Spanish Caprice') and the *Russian Easter Festival* overture. He also undertook completion or revision of the work of several of his colleagues, notably of Mussorgsky's *Boris Godunov* and Borodin's *Prince Igor*.

Rossini, Gioacchino (1792–1868).
Italian composer of operas, serious and comic, in the *bel canto* style of his time. A particularly striking feature of his music consists of the gradual building-up of a small but significant phrase into a splendid climax, a custom which earned him the title of 'Signor Crescendo'. His operas include *La Scala di seta* ('The Silken Ladder'), *La Gazza ladra* ('The Thieving Magpie'), *La Cenerentola* ('Cinderella'), *Semiramide, The Barber of Seville* (which has some of the same characters as Mozart's 'The Marriage of Figaro', but not the same plot), and *William Tell* (based on Friedrich Schiller's play about the legendary Swiss hero). This opera, written for the Paris stage, was also his last. From the time of its successful production until his death nearly forty years later, Rossini lived in semi-retirement in Paris. The few further works he did produce, such as the songs and duets published as *Soirées Musicales* ('Musical Evenings'), he humorously called 'sins of my old age'.

Ruggles, Carl (1876–1971).
American composer who created a strongly individual style in such works as the symphonic poems *Men and Mountains* and *Sun-Treader*, and *Angels* for six trumpets. He was also a painter.

Camille Saint-Saëns

Saint-Saëns, Camille (1835–1921). French organist, pianist and composer. He composed in a generally clear and melodious style, and in practically every existing musical form. Many of his largest works—his operas and three symphonies (no 3 with organ)—are not regularly performed today; but others remain favourite concert pieces such as the *Danse Macabre*; and the humorous *Le Carnaval des animaux* ('The Carnival of the Animals', subtitled 'grand zoological fantasy') for two pianos and orchestra, which includes the piece called 'The Swan'.

Sarasate, Pablo de (1844–1908). Spanish violinist and one of the greatest virtuoso players of his time. He also composed a number of violin works and had others written specially for him, notably the 'Spanish' Symphony (really a concerto) by the French composer Edouard Lalo.

Satie, Erik (1866–1925). French composer, though his mother was Scottish. He composed mainly for the piano, producing, in works like the three pieces called *Gymnopédie*, music of typically French elegance and refinement. Other pieces, with such startling titles as *Trois Morceaux en forme de poire* ('Three Pear-shaped Pieces') and *Embryons desséchés* ('Dried-up Embryos'), represent his strong reaction against the heavy, emotional character of late Romantic music; and in this respect he had considerable influence on the group of young French composers known as 'Les Six'. He did, however, write one quite 'serious' work, a type of cantata called *Socrate*, based on Plato's writings.

Scarlatti, Alessandro (1660–1725). Italian composer of many masses, cantatas, madrigals, also much instrumental music, but now chiefly remembered for his operas, whose style influenced Handel and many other eighteenth-century operatic composers. His son **Domenico** (1685–1757) also wrote some operas, but his most important works are reckoned to be his keyboard sonatas (over 500 in number), which made a big contribution to the development of Classical sonata form. Many of these sonatas (or 'exercises' as they were often called in Domenico Scarlatti's own lifetime) are delightful pieces in their own right; one of them is nicknamed 'Cat's Fugue'.

Schnabel, Artur (1882–1951). Austrian pianist who settled in the United States after the Nazis came to power. His playing marked an end to the grand Romantic style and the start of a much more controlled style of performance. Beethoven was his speciality.

Schoenberg, Arnold (1874–1951). Austrian composer who worked first in Germany then, after the Nazi rise to power, in the United States. His early compositions, such as *Verklärte Nacht* ('Transfigured Night') and *Gurrelieder* ('Songs of Gurra', for solo singers, chorus and orchestra) are written in a heavily late Romantic, post-Wagnerian style. It was Schoenberg's reaction against this style, and his creation of an entirely new method of composition, called twelve-tone, dodecaphonic or serial composition, that made him one of the most influential figures in twentieth-century music. Works moving towards this new style, or employing it to a greater or lesser extent, include *Erwartung* ('Expectation'), which is like a short opera for one character; the cantata *A Survivor from Warsaw* (about Nazi crimes against Jews); the unfinished opera *Moses and Aaron*; also some

157

orchestral, instrumental and piano pieces. Schoenberg's originality and influence went further with his song-cycle called *Pierrot Lunaire* ('Moonstruck Pierrot'), in which he first used in a fully developed form a performing style called *Sprechgesang* ('speech-song'). In this, as the term suggests, the singer hovers half-way between speaking and singing.

Schubert, Franz (1797–1828). Austrian composer who lived and died in Vienna and received almost no recognition during his own short lifetime. Some of his music was only rediscovered years after his death. Schubert continued the so-called Viennese tradition of Haydn, Mozart and Beethoven; he composed nine symphonies—no 4 in C minor is called 'Tragic', no 8 in B minor is the so-called 'Unfinished' because it has only two movements, no 9 in C major is called 'the Great C major'—also a string quintet, string quartets and piano sonatas in a basically Classical form; plus many short piano pieces such as the Impromptus and the group called *Moments Musicaux* ('Musical Moments'). But it is as a composer of *Lieder* (songs) that he is generally regarded as the first great figure of Romantic music. Schubert wrote over six hundred songs—all to existing poems—some rarely performed, others among the best-loved pieces in all music. Famous individual *Lieder* are: 'Heidenröslein' ('Wayside Rose'), 'Gretchen am Spinnrade' ('Gretchen at the Spinning-Wheel'), 'Der Erlkönig, ('The Erl King') and 'An die Musik' ('To Music'). Greatest are the song-cycles *Die schöne Müllerin* ('The Fair Maid of the Mill') and *Die Winterreise* ('The Winter Journey'); also the group of *Lieder* published posthumously under the title *Schwanengesang* ('Swan Song'). Schubert used some of his *Lieder* again in instrumental compositions, notably in the 'Trout' Quintet and in the String Quartet in D minor, 'Death and the Maiden'. There are also the overture and incidental music

to the play *Rosamunde*, though the overture that now goes under that title was originally intended for a different stage work. Schubert's works have been catalogued by the scholar Otto Deutsch and are often quoted with their 'Deutsch' or 'D' number.

Schuman, William (born 1910). American composer, many of whose works are inspired by some aspect of native American music, including jazz. Among these are *A William Billings Overture* and *New England Triptych* (both using themes by the early American composer William Billings) and the *American Festival Overture*. Other compositions include eight symphonies, a piano and a violin concerto and the opera *The Mighty Casey*, which has baseball as its theme.

Franz Schubert as a very young man.

Robert Schumann

Schumann, Robert (1810–56). German composer of some of the finest Romantic music, especially for the piano—*Papillons* ('Butterflies'), *Carnaval* (based on the notes which correspond, in German, to the letters of a place name connected with the composer's private life), *Kreisleriana* (inspired by a character from the stories of E.T.A. Hoffmann), *Kinderscenen* ('Scenes of Childhood') and *Davidsbündler-Tänze* ('Dances of the League of David', inspired by Schumann's imaginary 'League of David', or group of progressive young musicians). He was also a great *Lieder* composer with his song-cycles *Dichterliebe* ('Poet's Love') and *Frauenliebe und -leben* ('Woman's Love and Life'). Other compositions include four symphonies—no 1 is the 'Spring', no 3 the 'Rhenish'—the very popular Piano Concerto in A minor, and chamber music. In addition, Schumann was a noted musical journalist and critic. His wife Clara (her maiden name was Wieck) was a brilliant pianist and composer in her own right. After Robert's tragic mental breakdown and death, she became one of Brahms's closest friends and musical colleagues.

Schütz, Heinrich (1585–1672). German composer who studied for some years with Giovanni Gabrieli in Venice, and was an important link between Italian music of the Renaissance and German music of the Baroque period. In particular, his settings of the Passion served as a model for Bach when he came to write his St John and St Matthew Passions.

Scriabin, Alexander (1872–1915). Russian pianist and composer who progressed from a Romantic, Chopin-like style of composition in his sonatas and other piano pieces to music of harmonic originality and daring. This was prompted by his deep interest in Theosophy, a kind of occult religion with a world-wide following during his lifetime.

Andrés Segovia

Scriabin devised what he called a 'mystic chord'—really a new kind of scale—using this in several orchestral works, including *Prometheus, the Poem of Fire*. He also invented a 'keyboard of colour' which related colours to notes and was intended to project these onto a screen; but it was never used.

Segovia, Andrés (born 1893). Spanish guitarist who has done more than anyone else to establish the guitar as a serious concert instrument.

His playing has inspired compositions from his fellow countryman Manuel de Falla and others.

Shaw, Artie (born 1910). American jazz clarinettist and band leader, and one of the biggest names during the swing era of the 1930s and 1940s. He recorded several times with Blues singer Billie Holiday, and made some of his most successful discs with an ensemble called The Gramercy Five, including 'Special Delivery Stomp' and 'Summit Ridge Drive'.

159

Shostakovich, Dmitri (1906–75). Soviet Russian composer, now honoured in his own country as one of the greatest Soviet artists, although there were times when his work was severely criticized by the authorities because it was considered too difficult and advanced, or not sufficiently patriotic in spirit. In fact, Shostakovich's career was constantly marked by his efforts to reconcile his own creative style with his duty as a Soviet artist to serve the needs of state and people. His largest body of music is contained in his fifteen symphonies, some of which carry a strong political or patriotic theme—no 7, the 'Leningrad' Symphony, was partly composed in that city during its terrible period of siege in the Second World War. Other works include concertos for various instruments, an important group of string quartets, and much piano music; also the opera originally called *Lady Macbeth of Mtsensk District* (soon after renamed *Katerina Ismailova*) which was one of the works that got him into political trouble.

Sibelius, Jean (1865–1957). Finnish composer, and his country's greatest musical figure. His most important works are his seven symphonies, which as a group show his progress towards a very distinctive orchestral style, noted for its economical, sometimes quite sparse scoring and concentration of ideas (the Seventh Symphony being condensed into one continuous and relatively short movement). From another point of view, these symphonies represent Sibelius's reaction against the heavy and complex orchestral style of post-Wagnerian composers like Mahler and Richard Strauss. Many people also consider them, and the Violin Concerto in D minor, to represent much of the character of his native land. Sibelius wrote other orchestral works which are more openly programmatic, such as the tone poems *En Saga, The Swan of*

Dmitri Shostakovich

Jean Sibelius

Tuonela and *Tapiola*, inspired by either the spirit or the imagery of Finnish myth and legend; also the early *Finlandia* which has become a kind of patriotic hymn. Another popular composition is the *Valse Triste*. Sibelius, like Rossini, suddenly stopped composing, producing virtually nothing more during the last thirty years of his life.

Skalkottas, Nikos (1904–49). Greek violinist and composer, a pupil and musical follower of Schoenberg, but also a nationalist composer in the way he made use of Greek folk songs and dances. He received very little recognition in his own lifetime, most of his compositions—the Greek Dances for orchestra, piano concertos and instrumental works—being published only after his death.

Smetana, Bedřich (1824–84). Bohemian-Czech pianist, conductor and composer, and founder of the Czech national style or school of music. As a conductor, he helped to establish a Czech national opera in Prague and became its leading musical figure. As a composer he made great use of Czech folk song

and dance, in his opera *The Bartered Bride*, and in his largest orchestral work *Ma Vlast* ('My Country' or 'My Fatherland'), which is a group of tone poems depicting different aspects of the Czech landscape or history. Like Beethoven, Smetana went deaf, alluding to this affliction in his String Quartet in E minor, called *From my Life*, by the use of a very high, bleak-sounding violin note.

Smith, Bessie (about 1896–1938). Jazz vocalist, who started her career with hot gospel and Blues singer Ma Rainey and became the most famous interpreter of the Blues. Her greatest period was during the 1920s, after which her style began to go out of fashion and personal problems affected her performance. Tragically, she died after a car accident.

Solti, Sir Georg (born 1912). Hungarian-born conductor, Musical Director of the Covent Garden Opera for ten years, also closely associated with several orchestras, including the Chicago Symphony Orchestra, and noted for the dynamic character of his performances. He is also a pianist.

John Philip Sousa

Karlheinz Stockhausen

Sousa, John Philip (1854–1932). American military band leader and composer. He raised playing standards in his own bands to a high professional level, and lived up to his own claim that 'a march should make a man with a wooden leg want to step out' by composing some of the very finest marches, including 'The Washington Post' and 'The Stars and Stripes Forever'. The sousaphone, a large brass wind instrument designed to encircle the player's body, is named after him.

Spohr, Ludwig (1784–1859). German violinist, conductor and composer. He produced a very large quantity of music—operas and oratorios, symphonies and concertos, and much chamber music—in a tuneful, Romantic style that made him for a long time one of the most popular of composers. He was a pioneer figure in the modern art of conducting, being among the first to use a baton.

Stamitz, Johann Wenzel (1717–57). Bohemian-born violinist and composer (the original version of his name being Stamič). He was Musical Director at the Court of Mannheim and founder of the so-called Mannheim School of musicians who contributed much to the development of the symphony, concerto, sonata and other eighteenth-century Classical forms. Johann and his son **Karl** (1745–1801) both composed symphonies and other works in the new Classical style of their time.

Still, William Grant (born 1895). American composer and the first black American to compose and conduct a large symphonic work— the 'Afro-American' Symphony. His other works include the opera *Troubled Island* (about Haiti), and *Lenox Avenue* for chorus and orchestra (portraying Harlem, the black quarter of New York).

Stockhausen, Karlheinz (born 1928). German composer and one of the most imaginative and inventive figures of late twentieth-century music. He has based some of his compositions on the twelve-tone methods of Schoenberg and Webern, made extensive use of electronic apparatus, and developed the possibilities of indeterminacy, which leaves certain options open to performers. His works include *Gruppen* for three orchestral groups, *Zyklus* for percussion players, *Kontakte* for electronic sounds, piano and percussion, *Hymnen* (being an electronic treatment of various national anthems), and *Stimmung* ('Tuning' or 'Atmosphere') for six voices electronically controlled. The first composer to publish a fully electronic score in the form of diagrams, Stockhausen is also a lively teacher and lecturer, especially on behalf of his own ideas and music.

161

Johann Strauss the Younger

Richard Strauss

Strauss, Johann, the elder
(1804–1849)
and **the younger** (1825–1899).
Austrian violinists, conductors and
composers. As father and son they
built up the waltz into the most popular dance of all time, and were enormously successful in the process. In
fact, Johann Strauss the elder is best
remembered today for his *Radetzky
March* (named after an Austrian
general), while it was his son who
wrote such famous waltzes as 'The
Blue Danube' and 'Tales from the
Vienna Woods'. Johann Strauss the
younger was equally successful in the
field of operetta, his masterpiece here
being *Die Fledermaus* ('The Bat'). His
brothers Eduard and Josef were also
composers of waltzes and other
dances such as the polka.

Strauss, Richard (1864–1949).
German composer, generally regarded as the last great figure in the
tradition of German Romantic
music. His early compositions were a
series of symphonic poems, written
for a very large post-Wagnerian
orchestra, which amazed the musical
world of the time with their vivid
and sometimes startling descriptive
effects. These include *Don Juan*, *Till
Eulenspiegel* (episodes in the life of a
German folk hero), *Also Sprach
Zarathustra* ('Thus Spake
Zarathustra', inspired by the writings
of the philosopher Nietzsche), *Don
Quixote* (based on the famous novel
by Cervantes), and *Ein Heldenleben*
('A Hero's Life', really an autobiog-
raphical study in music). Strauss then
turned his attention to opera. *Salome*
(based on Oscar Wilde's play, not the
Bible) and *Elektra* (from the play by
Sophocles) shocked early audiences
with their lurid scenes and accompanying music. *Der Rosenkavalier*
('The Cavalier of the Rose', a love
story set in eighteenth-century
Vienna) marked the high point of his
collaboration with the librettist
Hugo von Hofmannsthal, and was his
greatest success. *Ariadne auf Naxos*
and other operas followed. He also
wrote many *Lieder* (songs), some with
orchestral accompaniment, and two
of the finest concertos for the horn.
Strauss remained, rather unhappily,
in Germany after the Nazis came to
power, and was ruined by the Second
World War.

Igor Stravinsky as a young man

Sir Arthur Sullivan

Stravinsky, Igor (1882–1971). Russian-born composer who lived in France for many years before finally settling in the United States and becoming an American citizen. He rose swiftly to fame in the years just before the First World War with the three progressively more brilliant and adventurous scores he produced for the Diaghilev Ballet—*The Firebird* (based on a Russian fairy tale), *Petrushka* (portraying the tragic existence of the traditional Russian puppet Petrushka, or 'Little Pete'), and *The Rite of Spring* (produced in France with the title *Le Sacre du printemps*, and portraying pagan rites in ancient Russia). The war put an end to such big productions, and Stravinsky started to compose on a much smaller scale—*The Soldier's Tale* (for three actors and a small jazz-style band), *Les Noces* ('The Wedding', for chorus and soloists, four pianos and percussion). He also entered his so-called 'Neo-Classical' period, composing such works as the Octet for Wind Instruments and the

opera-oratorio *Oedipus Rex* (based on a play by Sophocles) in a very cool, unemotional style. The Symphony of Psalms, Symphony in Three Movements, the opera *The Rake's Progress* (inspired by Hogarth's series of paintings of the same name) and other works mark his gradual return to a more expressive style; and in his final group of works, including further ballet scores, he made use of twelve-tone methods of composition. Like his almost exact contemporary, the artist Pablo Picasso, Stravinsky's creative life passed through a number of distinct periods or styles, and he remained one of music's most influential figures during the first half of this century and beyond.

Sullivan, Sir Arthur (1842–1900). English organist, conductor and composer who helped to re-establish the name of English music and musicians after a long period of decline, with his symphony, cantata *The Golden Legend* and several other

'serious' works. It was, however, his long partnership with the librettist W.S. Gilbert that has won him lasting fame. Their tremendously successful series of comic operettas include *Trial by Jury*, *HMS Pinafore*, *The Pirates of Penzance*, *Patience*, *Iolanthe*, *Ruddigore*, *The Mikado*, *The Yeomen of the Guard* and *The Gondoliers*. Music from them has been used in the ballet *Pineapple Poll* which is based on a story by Gilbert.

Suppé, Franz von (1819–95). Austrian composer of many once-popular operettas, the overture to *Light Cavalry* still being a popular concert piece. Another is the overture he wrote to the play *Poet and Peasant*.

Sutherland, Joan (born 1926). Australian operatic soprano who has gained a world-wide reputation for her singing of the great *bel canto* roles, mainly in the operas of Bellini and Donizetti.

Sweelinck, Jan Pieterszoon
(1562–1621).
Dutch organist and composer. He greatly advanced organ technique in his compositions, especially in the writing of fugues for the instrument, and had a big influence on the development of organ music in Holland and Germany up to the time of Bach. Like Schütz, he studied in Venice for a time, and this inspired him to write some fine choral music also.

Tallis, Thomas (about 1505–85). English organist and composer. With his younger colleague William Byrd, Tallis lived through the very disturbed religious period of English history that involved the break with the authority of the Pope and eventual establishment of the Anglican Church. Despite these troubles, he composed religious music, to texts both in Latin and in English, of great solemnity and polyphonic skill. His Latin motet *Spem in alium* is, in fact, one of the high points in the whole history of polyphonic music, being written for eight small choirs of five voices each, and having forty separate parts. As one of the most eminent musicians of his time, Tallis shared with Byrd the sole right to print music in England.

Tartini, Giuseppe (1692–1770). Italian violinist and composer. He was a great innovator in the field of violin construction and playing technique, especially with regard to the design and use of new kinds of bow. He also wrote some important books on musical theory and the physics of acoustics. As a composer, Tartini is best remembered for his so-called 'Devil's Trill' Sonata, said to have been inspired by a dream in which the Devil appeared before him playing the violin.

Tatum, Arthur or 'Art' (1910–56). American jazz pianist. He raised jazz playing standards to a virtuoso level which amazed such fellow pianists as

Peter Ilich Tchaikovsky

Walter Gieseking and Vladimir Horowitz when they first heard him. He had, at the same time, a subtle and often complex rhythmic sense and a feeling for harmonies sometimes reminiscent of Debussy. Almost blind since childhood, Art Tatum maintained the same brilliant standards from the late 1920s right up to the year of his death, and his influence on other jazz pianists, such as the Canadian Oscar Peterson, has been immense.

Taverner, John (about 1495–1545). English composer who was appointed by Cardinal Wolsey to the post of organist and choirmaster at what is now Christ Church Cathedral, Oxford, and produced some of the finest English Latin church music, including eight settings of the Mass. Later in life his conversion to Protestantism and his part in the break-up of the English monasteries diverted him from music.

Tchaikovsky, Peter Ilich
(1840–93).
The first Russian composer to become internationally famous and one of the most popular of all the great composers. His success took him on concert tours of Europe and the United States, but he remained a basically unhappy man, disturbed by personal problems. His long association (virtually all by correspondence) with his private patron Madame Nadezhda von Meck was a big source of encouragement as well as financial security, and it was a great blow to his feelings when she broke it off. He died after drinking untreated water during an outbreak of cholera in St Petersburg. Tchaikovsky's music, though typically Russian in some respects, is less consciously so than that of his nationalist colleagues known as 'The Five'. He composed mostly in established musical forms, like the symphony and concerto, adding to them his own special gifts for dramatic orchestration and grand melody, together with a fair degree of personal expression—all in the late Romantic manner of his day. His principal works are: six symphonies—no 1 ('Winter Daydreams'), no 2 ('Little Russian'), no 3 ('Polish'), no 6 ('Pathétique'); also the 'Manfred' Symphony (based on the subject of a poem by Byron); three piano concertos (no 1 in B flat minor being the famous one); a violin concerto; the symphonic poems (or fantasy-overtures) *Romeo and Juliet*, *Hamlet* and *Francesca da Rimini* (based on the poetry of Dante); the operas *Eugene Onegin* and *The Queen of Spades*; the three celebrated ballet scores to *Swan Lake*, *The Sleeping Beauty* and *The Nutcracker*; and the overture *1812*.

Telemann, Georg Philipp
(1681–1767).
German composer whose output—very large even by the prolific standards of his time—includes about forty operas, forty oratorios, six hundred orchestral works and many

Sir Michael Tippett

more instrumental and vocal pieces. His music is of interest because it marks the transition from the early eighteenth-century Baroque style of Bach and Handel to the later eighteenth-century Rococo and Classical styles of Haydn and Mozart. A very successful man, he was for some years director of music in the City of Hamburg.

Thomson, Virgil (born 1896).
American composer who studied in Europe, but has made frequent use of traditional American music, such as the old revivalist hymn tunes, in his own works. These include the operas *Four Saints in Three Acts* and *The Mother of Us All* (both with librettos by the famous writer Gertrude Stein). He has also been an eminent music critic.

Tippett, Sir Michael Kemp
(born 1905).
English composer who, like his compatriots Vaughan Williams and Benjamin Britten, has sometimes linked his own music to great English music of past times. He has also made use of Negro spirituals and jazz. His works include the operas *The Midsummer Marriage*, *King Priam* and *The Knot Garden*, the oratorio *A Child of our Time*, symphonies, string quartets and other instrumental compositions, and song-cycles.

Torelli, Giuseppe (1658–1709).
Italian violinist and composer who, with his fellow countryman Corelli, was one of the pioneer figures in the development of the concerto grosso and other new musical forms for the violin family of instruments.

165

Arturo Toscanini

Vaughan Williams, Ralph
(1872–1958).
English composer whose main
sources of inspiration were English
folk music and English music of past
times, giving much of his own music
a distinctive, nationalistic sound. His
compositions include nine
symphonies—no 1 ('Sea'), no 2
('London'), no 3 ('Pastoral') and no 7
(*Sinfonia Antartica*, taken from his
score to the film *Scott of the Antarctic*);
Fantasia on a Theme of Thomas
Tallis; overture to Aristophanes' play
The Wasps; the opera *Pilgrim's
Progress* (after the novel by John
Bunyan); the ballet *Job*
(inspired by William Blake's illustrations to the Book of Job); *The Lark
Ascending* for violin and orchestra; the
song-cycle *On Wenlock Edge* (to
poems by A.E. Housman); and many
folk song arrangements, notably the
Fantasia on 'Greensleeves'.

Verdi, Giuseppe (1813–1901).
Italian operatic composer. He was
born in the northern Italian district of
Parma, and the background to most
of his career was the long campaign
leading to a politically united Italy.
When he died, in Milan, he was
beloved as a person and revered,
through his music, as one of the
greatest heroes of his country. He
progressed slowly but surely as a
composer, his work constantly
gaining in assurance and dramatic
force, until he had created a style of
continuous musical and dramatic
development quite similar in some
respects to Wagner's music-drama.
His most famous operas are: *Rigoletto*
(based on a play by Victor Hugo), *La
Traviata* (which can be translated as
'The Woman Gone Astray', and is
based on a novel and play by
Alexandre Dumas the younger),*Il
Trovatore* ('The Troubadour'), *Simon
Boccanegra*, *Un Ballo in Maschera* ('A
Masked Ball'), *La Forza del Destino*
('The Force of Destiny'), *Don Carlos*,
Aida (intended to celebrate the
opening of the Suez Canal), *Otello*
and *Falstaff* (these last two

Toscanini, Arturo (1867–1957).
Italian conductor, renowned for his
attention to detail and for the drive
and power of his performances. He
was also one of the first to conduct
regularly without a score, a habit
prompted in his case by extreme
short-sightedness. He was already a
world-famous figure when the
National Broadcasting Company
(NBC) Symphony Orchestra was
specially created for him in New
York, and he made some of his most
celebrated recordings with them.
Included among them are his
dynamic interpretations of the
Beethoven symphonies.

Varèse, Edgar (1885–1965).
French-born composer who lived
and worked mainly in the United
States. He was a very advanced
musical thinker, exploring many new
sound possibilities, including the use
of electronic instruments, ahead of
most of his colleagues. He also gave
some of his compositions unusual
scientific sounding titles, such as
Density 21.5 (a piece for solo flute) and
Ionization (for percussion instruments). Varèse expressed his own
attitude to his work as a so-called
avant-garde composer by saying 'an
artist is never ahead of his time. Most
people are behind theirs!'

Ralph Vaughan Williams—portrait by Sir Gerald Kelly

Shakespearian adaptations being the fruit of Verdi's collaboration with Arrigo Boito as librettist). Verdi also composed a famous setting of the Requiem Mass, prompted by the death of his friend, the writer Alessandro Manzoni.

Victoria, Tomás Luis de
(about 1548–1611).
Spanish composer who lived in Italy for many years (and for this reason is sometimes known as Vittoria). He wrote only church music, and its deeply devotional character is often compared with the music of Palestrina, whom he knew in Rome.

Villa-Lobos, Heitor (1887–1959).
Brazilian pianist and the most famous Latin American composer. He wrote a very large amount of music: operas, ballets, symphonies, concertos, and the well-known *Bachianas Brasileiras*, which are pieces for various instrumental and vocal groups combining something of the spirit of Bach with traditional Brazilian songs and dances. He also composed some very imaginative and beautiful music for the guitar.

Vitry, Philippe de (1291–1361).
French poet, priest, court official and composer. Only a few examples of his music survive, but he has a significant place in musical history on account of his treatise explaining new styles of composition which he was probably the first to call *ars nova*, or the 'New Art'.

Vivaldi, Antonio
(about 1678–1741).
Italian priest, violinist and composer who spent much of his life teaching music at a girls' orphanage in Venice, though he died in Vienna. He built upon the work of his older compatriots Corelli and Torelli, writing well over four hundred works in the concerto grosso style, the most famous of these being his very descriptive set of four concertos with a part for solo violin called *The Four*

Richard Wagner

Seasons. Known as 'The Red Priest' because of the colour of his hair, Vivaldi also composed operas and oratorios. Bach admired and arranged some of his music.

Wagner, Richard (1813–83).
German composer, born in Leipzig, who revolutionized opera, orchestration and harmony, and also strongly influenced the artistic and philosophical thought of his time. His greatest single aim was the creation of what he considered a new art form called 'music drama'. By force of will, and with other people's money, he achieved his ambitions, also planning and seeing built a special theatre for his operas and music-dramas at Bayreuth in Bavaria. His second wife Cosima (Liszt's daughter, who divorced the conductor Hans von Bülow to marry him) and their two sons presided over the Bayreuth Festival until well into this century. Wagner himself died in Venice. His early operas include *Rienzi* (in its original version the

Fats Waller

longest of all his single operas but not typical of his subsequent work), *Der fliegende Holländer* ('The Flying Dutchman'), *Tannhäuser* (based on the life of a medieval German minstrel-knight) and *Lohengrin* (inspired by legends of the Holy Grail). After that he started work on what turned out to be his greatest realization of music drama: *Der Ring des Nibelungen* ('The Ring of the Nibelungs'), a cycle of four operas based on Teutonic myths and legends—*Das Rheingold* ('The Rhinegold'), *Die Walküre* ('The Valkyries'), *Siegfried* and *Götterdämmerung* ('Twilight of the Gods'). The other music dramas of his maturity are *Tristan und Isolde* (a love story from Celtic legend), *Die Meistersinger von Nürnberg* ('The

Mastersingers of Nuremberg', an evocation of the art and culture of Renaissance Germany), and *Parsifal* (based on another aspect of the Holy Grail legends, Parsifal being Lohengrin's father). A popular orchestral piece is the *Siegfried Idyll*, based on music from the opera *Siegfried*, which Wagner composed to celebrate the birth of his son—Siegfried!

Waller, Thomas Wright 'Fats' (1904–43).
American jazz pianist and songwriter. 'Fats' Waller was one of the most colourful and entertaining figures in jazz, a large man almost always pictured with a bowler hat perched jauntily on his head. He was a fine pianist with an immaculate

sense of swing, at his best accompanying himself in some of the songs that helped to make him famous—'Honeysuckle Rose' and 'Ain't Misbehavin'. The son of a church minister, he also sometimes played the organ or harmonium in a clever jazz style.

Walther von der Vogelweide (about 1170–1230).
Greatest of the medieval German poet-musicians known as *Minnesinger* ('Singers of Love'), whose songs were generally more serious and scholarly than those of the troubadours and *trouvères* of Provence and France. He is portrayed in Wagner's opera *Tannhäuser*, which is the story of another German poet-musician or minstrel-knight of the Middle Ages.

169

Sir William Walton—portrait by Michael Ayrton

Walton, Sir William (born 1902). English composer, not so interested in English folk music and literature as Vaughan Williams and Britten, developing instead a strong, bright orchestral style and sometimes influenced by jazz. His works include *Façade* (originally composed to accompany poems by Edith Sitwell, now better known either as a ballet or as a full-scale orchestral suite), two symphonies, the concert overtures *Portsmouth Point* and *Scapino*, the opera *Troilus and Cressida*, and the oratorio *Belshazzar's Feast*; also film music.

Weber, Carl Maria von (1786–1826).
German conductor and composer. His operas *Der Freischütz* ('The Marksman'), *Euryanthe* and *Oberon* were very important in the development of German Romantic opera, and influenced Wagner. He also wrote some fine orchestral and instrumental music, notably for the clarinet, and the well-known *Invitation to the Dance* (originally a piano piece, later orchestrated by Berlioz). Like Chopin he had poor health and died relatively young from consumption.

Webern, Anton von (1883–1945). Austrian composer. Together with Alban Berg, he was Schoenberg's principal musical disciple, developing his own style based on twelve-tone methods of composition. The outstanding feature of his style is extreme brevity and economy of notes, great significance being attached to every single note or sound in a piece. His actual compositions are also few in number, but of importance to twentieth-century music. They can be regarded as the final and complete reaction against the massive late Romantic orchestral works of Mahler, Richard Strauss and others. Webern was accidentally shot dead by an Allied soldier at the end of the Second World War.

Weelkes, Thomas
(about 1575–1623).
English organist and composer of church music, some instrumental pieces for viols, and many madrigals. With other Elizabethan madrigalists he contributed to *The Triumphs of Oriana*.

Weill, Kurt (1900–50).
German composer who settled in the United States after the Nazi rise to power. His fame rests with the satiri-

cal, jazz-style operas he produced in collaboration with the dramatist Berthold Brecht—*Die Drei-groschenoper* ('The Threepenny Opera', being an adaptation of the eighteenth-century English stage piece *The Beggar's Opera*), and *The Rise and Fall of the City of Mahagonny*. The well-known song 'Mack the Knife' comes from the first of these.

Wilbye, John (1574–1638).
English composer of some of the finest madrigals of the Elizabethan period, contributing to the famous collection published as *The Triumphs of Oriana*. He composed very little else.

Willaert, Adriaan
(about 1490–1562).
Flemish composer who was Director of Music at St Mark's, Venice. In this capacity he created the antiphonal styles of music—contrasting one group of singers or instrumentalists with another—which Andrea and Giovanni Gabrieli developed further and which made Venice such an influential centre of Renaissance and early Baroque music. He also composed some of the first true madrigals.

Williamson, Malcolm (born 1931).
Australian composer who has worked mainly in Britain. His works include the opera *Our Man in Havana* (based on Graham Greene's satirical novel about the Secret Service) and the large-scale choral and orchestral Mass of Christ the King.

Wolf, Hugo (1860–1903).
Austrian composer, mainly of songs which are considered among the finest in the tradition of German Romantic *Lieder*. There are three important groups of these, *The Italian Song Book*, *The Spanish Song Book* and the *Mörike Songs* (to words by the German poet G.F. Mörike). Other songs are to poems by Goethe. Wolf also wrote one opera, *Der Corregidor* (set in Spain), and the *Italian Serenade* for string quartet (which he later orchestrated). He died insane.

Xenakis, Iannis (born 1922).
Greek composer who has introduced many new ideas into music, including the use of mathematical formulae and computers in composition.

Ysaÿe, Eugène (1858–1931).
World-famous Belgian violinist, also a conductor and composer mainly of concertos and other works for the violin.

Carl Maria von Weber

171

Musical Forms and Terms

Absolute Music
Music that is supposed to express no thought or idea beyond the music itself; the exact opposite of descriptive programme music.

Absolute Pitch (or Perfect Pitch)
The ability to identify the PITCH of a note or the KEY of a piece of music by ear alone.

Accelerando
Italian tempo marking, meaning 'accelerate, speed up'.

Accidental
The sharpening or flattening of a particular note not accounted for in the KEY signature of a piece; or the temporary naturalizing of a note that is sharpened or flattened according to the key signature.

Adagio
Italian tempo marking, meaning 'slow'. Thus *adagio maestoso*, 'slow and majestic'.

Aleatory
Derived from the Latin word *alea* meaning 'dice', it describes music in which the composer has introduced an element of chance into the performance. The term is often taken to include music that invites the performers to decide for themselves when and at what point in the score to start or stop playing, though strictly speaking this is a matter of *indeterminacy* and not quite the same.

Allegro
Italian tempo marking, meaning 'fairly fast'. Thus *allegro con brio*, 'fairly fast and with spirit'; *allegro ma non troppo*, 'steady and not too fast'. *Allegretto* means 'little allegro', or 'not quite so fast'.

Alto
1) The range of pitch of a boy's voice, deeper than treble, or the pitch of a man's voice singing falsetto (a counter-tenor);
2) the range of pitch of an instrument within a particular family of instruments (e.g. alto saxophone);
3) the name of a CLEF.

Andante
Italian tempo marking, meaning 'at a leisurely pace'. Thus *andante cantabile*, 'leisurely and in a singing style'.

Anthem
1) A piece of church choral music dating back in name and style to the establishment of the Church of England and taking the place of the older Roman Catholic Latin MOTET;
2) any fairly solemn piece of choral or vocal music, like national anthems.

Antiphonal
From the Greek word meaning 'sounding across', it describes music intended to be performed by separate groups of singers or instrumentalists so as to produce a kind of stereophonic effect. An *antiphon* is a piece of church music that usually includes alternative passages for a solo singer and a whole choir, or alternative passages for two separate choirs.

Arco
Italian for 'bow', telling players of stringed instruments to start using their bows again after playing PIZZICATO.

Aria
Italian for 'song', mainly used to describe the fairly substantial and often technically difficult songs of opera and oratorio.

Arpeggio
From the Italian *arpa*, 'harp', it describes the method of spreading out the notes of a chord one after the other, almost always from the bottom note upwards, as they are usually played on the harp.

Atonal Music
Music not written in any of the major or minor keys. Some of Wagner's music verges on atonality; pioneer figures of twentieth-century music, such as Debussy and Bartók, also developed atonal styles of composition; but the term is most closely associated with Schoenberg's TWELEVE-TONE methods of compostion.

Aubade
French for a 'morning song'; *alborado* is the equivalent Spanish word sometimes used.

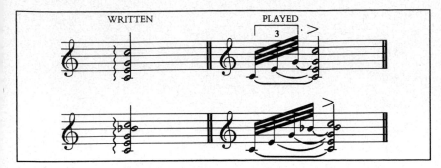

Chords to be played in an arpeggio style are written with a wavy line against them, as shown. This example also shows how to play them.

Ayre
English name for a type of song dating from about the end of the sixteenth century. The more up-to-date spelling is *air*.

Bagatelle
French word meaning 'trifle', and a name for fairly short, not too weighty pieces of music, usually for the piano; but Beethoven's bagatelles are more than just trifles.

Ballad
Type of song usually connected with a narrative poem (i.e. a poem recounting a story). Many traditional ballads are folk songs dating back, in various forms, hundreds of years. A *ballade*, the French version of the word, was used by Chopin and others as a title for piano pieces of a vaguely descriptive character.

Ballet
Combination of music and dancing. Examples of this can be found in most tribal societies, while in the ancient world the Greeks sometimes included dancing and music as a part of their drama. But ballet as we think of it today originated in Renaissance Italy and reached its first period of artistic importance in seventeenth-century France, at the court of Louis XIV. *Opéra-ballet* was basically opera with ballet sequences (a feature of much French opera), while *ballet-pantomime* was closer to true ballet, with no singing. Thus the traditional home of ballet is France, and though some of the finest ballet companies and ballet scores have been Russian, the names of the various dance steps and other technical terms are all in French. *Choreography* is the art of planning and creating ballet steps and routines, and the choreographer is the most important person in any ballet production. Some famous ballets (e.g. *Coppélia*, *Swan Lake*, *The Nutcracker*, *Petrushka*, *The Three-Cornered Hat*) have had music specially written for them. Others (e.g. *Les Sylphides*, *Façade*, *Pineapple Poll*) have music taken from some other source.

Bar
A small section of music. Most Western music is divided up into bars according to a regular rhythmic beat, though it is quite possible to change the rhythm from one bar to the next. The American name is *measure*.

Barcarolle
French word for a boating song, especially associated with Venetian gondolas. Chopin and Offenbach (in *The Tales of Hoffmann*) wrote barcarolles.

Baritone
1) The range of pitch of a man's voice, deeper than TENOR, not so deep as BASS;
2) the range of pitch of an instrument within a particular family of instruments (e.g. baritone saxophone).

Bass
1) The deepest range of pitch of a man's voice;
2) the deepest-pitched type of instrument within a particular family of instruments (e.g. bass viol);
3) the name of a CLEF.

Bel Canto
Italian for 'beautiful song', describing an operatic style of singing originally concerned with a refined and beautiful vocal tone, but meaning also singing of great agility and control.

Bebop
Jazz style which led to most other modern or 'progressive' jazz styles. The name (sometimes shortened to bop) suggests the generally restless, urgent character of the music.

Berceuse
French name for a lullaby or cradle song, given to some instrumental pieces.

Blues
Early and basic jazz style, a type of sung lament divided into sections of twelve bars with set harmonies. Other jazz, dance and pop music forms have developed from it. Composers and song-writers have loosely applied the name to pieces of a general jazz-like character.

Boogie Woogie
Jazz piano style like a kind of speeded-up Blues with a strong OSTINATO left-hand part.

Breve
Name for what was originally the note of briefest duration, but is today the note of longest duration and rarely used. The American name is *double-whole-note*.

Cadence
A kind of harmonic punctuation mark, usually consisting of two chords. According to the established rules of harmony, some types of cadence bring a piece of music to a

satisfactory close (like the *plagal cadence* which forms the 'amen' at the end of hymns), while others lead the music in new directions.

Cadenza

The Italian word for 'cadence', which also describes the section of a concerto movement reserved for the soloist. Originally the composer usually left a gap in the music, during which the soloist was supposed to improvize upon the tunes already heard; but most soloists today plan their cadenzas ahead of performance. In any event, since Beethoven many concertos have had their cadenzas written in by the composer.

Canon

A type of composition, rather like a ROUND, in which each voice or instrumental part enters in turn with the same melody, following each other round until the piece is brought to a satisfactory end.

Cantata

From the Italian *cantare* 'to sing', a composition for voices, usually with orchestra. Cantatas may be for a choir, for a choir and soloists or, more rarely, for one or two soloists only. They may be religious or secular.

Canticle

Type of religious hymn with words taken from the Bible except the Psalms.

Canzona

Type of medieval Italian poem and musical settings of it; but also the name sometimes given to an instrumental piece. *Canzonet* or *canzonetta*, 'little canzona', is a light and easy kind of song.

Capriccio

Italian for 'fancy' or 'whim', describing a generally light-hearted or delicately written piece of music. The French word is *caprice*.

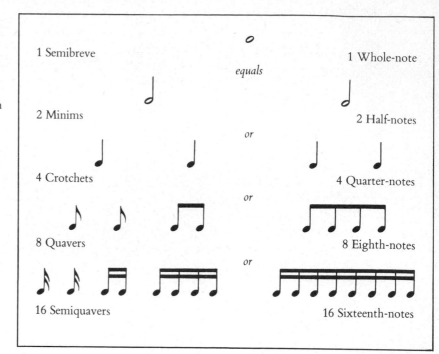

The relative duration of notes. From semibreve down to semiquaver, each type of note is equal to half the duration of the one above.

Carol

Religious song for ordinary people to sing, as opposed to trained singers; now mainly associated with Christmas, though there are carols for other festivals.

Cavatina

Italian word for a fairly short operatic aria; also sometimes applied to a song-like instrumental piece.

Chaconne

Originally a courtly dance, better known as a type of composition in variation form, in which a simple theme or motif repeated in the bass (called a ground bass) provides a basis for variations. Chaconnes may be vocal, but the form is best known as an instrumental one.

Chamber Music (Room Music)

The term grew up during the seventeenth and eighteenth centuries to describe instrumental music for small groups of players intended for the more informal atmosphere of a private room than for church, opera house or other public place. Though it has kept this meaning, it more specially describes the smaller instrumental forms that developed during the Classical period of the eighteenth century—the trio (piano, violin, cello), string quartet, string quintet and similar groups. By convention, music for one or two instruments is not usually classed as chamber music. We speak of a chamber music concert, but of a piano or violin recital.

Chanson

French for 'song', especially the name for a type of medieval or Renaissance French song for one or more voices, perhaps with instruments.

Charleston

Lively type of dance, developed out of early jazz, that was very popular in the United States and Europe during the 1920s.

The five clefs, showing how each is related to the same note, middle C. The treble and bass clefs are the most familiar ones today.

Chorale
Traditional type of German hymn tune, specially associated with the Lutheran Church. A *chorale-prelude* is an instrumental piece, usually for the organ, based on a chorale tune.

Chord
Two or more notes of different pitch sounded together.

Chromatic Scale
Progression of notes going up or down in pitch by a SEMITONE between each note, and therefore different from any of the major or minor scales. Obtained on a piano by playing both the white and black keys in succession.

Clef
In staff notation the sign that governs the pitch of notes written on or between the STAVE lines. There are five clefs, SOPRANO, TREBLE, ALTO, TENOR and BASS. The treble and bass clefs are the most widely used.

Coda
Italian for 'tail', describing an extra passage of music added to the end of a piece to round it off.

Coloratura
Italian word describing, usually in the case of a SOPRANO, a singer with a specially agile voice.

Concerto
Italian word for an orchestral composition with a major part for one, two or possibly three instrumental soloists.

The Classical concerto of Mozart's time had three movements, and with only a few exceptions this arrangement has been followed since. A *concerto for orchestra*, of which there are several examples this century, gives prominence to each instrumental group in the orchestra in turn.

Concerto Grosso
Italian for 'great concerto', an earlier form than the true concerto, most often composed for a string orchestra and a smaller group of string soloists, passages for the full orchestra (*ripieno*, 'replenished' or 'full') being contrasted with those for the soloists (*concertino*, 'little concert' or 'little group').

Conductus
Early type of POLYPHONIC composition for a choir. One singer declaimed a *cantus firmus* (Latin, 'fixed song'), around which the other parts were added. The origin of the name may be connected with religious processions, when priests, or effigies, were conducted from place to place.

Consort
Performance by a group of instrumentalists all playing instruments of the same family, e.g. viols or recorders, very popular in Renaissance times. A *broken consort* combined stringed and wind instruments.

Continuo
A continuous musical part in a work, usually for a keyboard instrument, designed to provide a lead or foundation to the performance; especially associated with seventeenth- and eighteenth-century orchestral music, but used also in some types of opera to aid the singers in RECITATIVE. Very often composers of the period in question directed performances of their own music by taking the continuo part. A *figured bass* was a kind of coded notation for continuo players, the figures indicating what chords and harmonies to play.

Contralto
The range of pitch of a woman's voice, deeper than SOPRANO.

Counterpoint
From the Latin *punctus contra punctum*, 'point against point' or 'note against note', a form of POLYPHONIC music in which two or more melodies, or different versions of the same melody, are played against each other, or interwoven note by note. The FUGUE is the greatest form of contrapuntal music.

Courante
French courtly dance, often used as the basis for a movement in eighteenth-century suites and other instrumental and orchestral music.

Crescendo (cresc.)
Italian dynamic marking, meaning 'get gradually louder'.

Crotchet
Note of duration, now used as the basis for many kinds of rhythm and tempo; the duration of other notes are usually measured against it. The American name is *quarter-note*.

Diatonic Music
Music written in one or other of the twenty-four major or minor keys; that is, most music written between about 1600 and 1900.

Diminuendo (dim.)
Italian dynamic marking, meaning 'get gradually softer'.

Dynamic markings in a passage from Debussy's Piano Prelude *Ondine*. Within each group of notes the music gets louder and softer again, as indicated.

Divertimento
Italian 'amusement', describing a fairly light and entertaining piece of instrumental music, usually in several movements. *Divertissement* is the French word.

Dodecaphonic Music
Greek word for 'twelve-tone' music, the method of composing, using all twelve notes of the CHROMATIC SCALE, invented by Schoenberg.

Dumka
A type of Slavonic song with alternative slow and sad, fast and happy, sections.

Duo
Music for two performers, usually referring to instrumentalists; but *duet* often means a song for two vocalists.

Dynamics
Aspect of musical performance concerned with degrees of loudness and softness.

Étude
French for 'study', a piece of instrumental music usually concerned with some aspect of playing technique.

Expressionism
Term mainly used in painting, but sometimes applied to music which is supposed to express the composer's inner or subconscious state of mind, as distinct from normal emotions. Some of Mahler's and Schoenberg's music could be called expressionist.

Fado
Type of Portuguese folk music.

Fandango
Lively Spanish dance, including castanets.

Fantasy
Name for a piece of music relatively free from any particular form and suggesting a mood of improvization. *Fantasia* and *fantaisie* are the respective Italian and French versions of the word.

Farandole
Old type of dance from Provence in southern France, traditionally for pipe and drum. Bizet's well-known farandole from his incidental music to *L'Arlésienne* is not in the correct rhythm, but is based on an old Provençal tune.

Flamenco
Type of Spanish song from Andalusia. There are various local styles, named after towns and cities of the region, e.g. the *Malagueña* and the *Sevillana*. One of the origins of flamenco is an old type of Spanish singing called *cante hondo* ('deep song'), rather sorrowful in character. The Arabic sound to the music also reminds us that Spain was occupied by the Moors of North Africa for hundreds of years.

Flat
Sign indicating that a note must be lowered in pitch by a SEMITONE.

Form
The way in which a piece of music is arranged or presented, based on many different factors, taken singly or in combination. The most important of these deal with the order in which tunes and other musical ideas are presented, the length of sections or of the whole piece reckoned in terms of bars or measures, the use of harmony, the use of rhythm. Form can also describe particular styles or methods of composition, such as the FUGUE or PASSACAGLIA.

Forte (f)
Italian dynamic marking, meaning 'loud'. *Fortissimo* (ff) means 'very loud'. *Mezzo-forte* (mf) means 'half loud', i.e. 'not too loud'.

Foxtrot
Type of American ballroom dance, very loosely based on jazz, which was popular both in America and Europe during the 1920s and 1930s.

Frequency
Term in the science of acoustics for the speed or rapidity of vibrations

giving rise to sound waves. Frequency is expressed in terms of the number of vibrations per second. It is directly related to PITCH, as any simple experiment with a stretched piece of string or elastic will show— the faster or higher the frequency, the higher the pitch of the sound.

Frottola
Italian song for several voices dating from about the beginning of the sixteenth century, and an early version of the MADRIGAL.

Fugue
The most developed form of COUNTERPOINT, in which a theme is first stated on its own, then added to in one or more versions or 'parts', and so built up into a closely interwoven musical structure. Bach and other composers of the Baroque period wrote fugues which were compositions in their own right. Later composers, notably Beethoven, sometimes included a type of fugue as part of a larger movement in a symphony, string quartet, sonata or other composition. The Italian term *fugato* means in a generally fugal style rather than a true fugue.

Galliard
Lively court dance of the fifteenth and sixteenth centuries.

Gavotte
Old type of dance sometimes included in instrumental suites of dances.

Glee
Type of English song for men's voices, popular in England during the eighteenth century, and then in the United States.

Gopak
Lively Russian folk dance.

Grave
Italian expression of mood, 'grave, solemn', often also meaning a slow tempo.

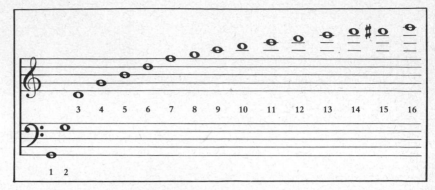

Harmonic series of a note. The fundamental, or leading note, is the lower G in the bass clef. The second harmonic is the G an octave above, the third is the D at an interval of a fifth above. The series continues upwards in pitch by progressively shorter intervals.

Harmonics (or Harmonic series)
The notes of different pitch that blend in various ways to make up any normal musical note, created by the fact that a vibrating string or column of air vibrates not only as a whole but in parts. The first and usually dominating note in a harmonic series is called the *fundamental*. The rest are *overtones*, or *upper partials*.

Harmony
That aspect of music concerned with blending notes and sequences of notes of different pitch.

Impromptu
Short instrumental piece, usually for the piano, in an improvizatory style.

Improvization
The art of composing music spontaneously. In the past it often meant improvizing on an existing theme, as Bach did, or improvizing on themes of a concerto movement in the CADENZA section reserved for the soloist. Much JAZZ is also improvized, within the framework of a form like the BLUES, or on the basis of a given tune.

Incidental Music
Music written in connection with a play or other stage work, to be played before, during and perhaps at the close of the performance. Much incidental music becomes best known in the concert hall in the form of overtures and suites.

Intermezzo
Italian for 'between' or 'in the middle', describing a piece of orchestral music to be played between the scenes of an opera; occasionally the name given to a short piece of instrumental music.

♯	✕	♭	♭♭	♮
sharp	double-sharp	flat	double-flat	natural

The signs for sharp, flat and natural. Double-sharp indicates the raising in pitch of a note by a whole tone; double-flat indicates the lowering in pitch of a note by the same tonal interval.

Interval
The 'distance' in pitch between two notes.

Invention
Name used by Bach for fairly short keyboard pieces, more fully called *two-part inventions* because they use two 'parts' or melodic lines in a contrapuntal way.

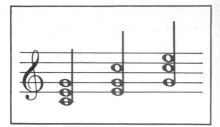

Simple chord inversions. Harmonically the chord remains the same, but the arrangement of the individual notes changes.

Inversion
1) A change in the placing of notes in a chord, according to pitch;
2) a melody played 'upside down', that is, with the relative pitch intervals between the notes reversed.

Jazz
The music primarily of black Americans, though there are many white jazz musicians also. Early or basic jazz forms—BLUES, RAGTIME, STOMPS, BOOGIE—are characterized by strong, syncopated rhythms (related to Latin American music), particular chords and harmonic sequences, and a large measure of IMPROVIZATION. Jazz later developed forms and styles, notably BEBOP, that considerably changed its original character. It also led to many dance music styles—SWING, ROCK N' ROLL.

Jig
A lively dance, associated especially with rural Britain. Under its French title of *gigue* it often forms a movement of instrumental dance suites.

American vocalist Ella Fitzgerald who has done much to popularize jazz singing. She is a noted scat singer (see page 184).

Jive
A very energetic way of dancing to swing and other jazz-inspired types of dance music.

Key
1) The most important factor in the HARMONY of much Western music written between about 1600 and the present day. The key to a piece of music is any one of the twenty-four major or minor SCALES on which the music is based; the *key-signature* at the beginning of a printed piece of music indicates which notes, if any, must be sharpened or flattened for the piece to conform to a particular scale. Changes of key mean moving the music from the harmonic context of one scale to another;
2) a lever which controls the mechanism for making one particular note sound in instruments like the piano and organ; the complete set of such keys forms a keyboard.

Ländler
Type of Austrian country dance, like a slow WALTZ. Mahler based some of his symphonic movements upon it.

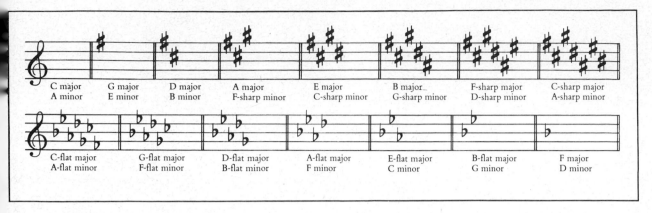

Key-signatures for the twenty-four major and minor keys. Each signature represents a major and its relative minor key.

Largo
Italian for 'broad', which can be a definite tempo marking for 'slow and stately', or indicate a mood corresponding to this. It is not really the name for a type of composition, despite Handel's 'Largo' (which he did not compose as such). *Larghetto*, 'little largo' meaning not quite so slow .

Ledger Line
In NOTATION, a short line or lines added above or below the normal stave lines to accommodate notes of extra high or low pitch.

Legato
Italian for 'bound together', describing a manner of performance whereby the notes are played without any sort of break to create a smooth, flowing effect.

Lento
Italian tempo marking, meaning 'slow'.

Lied
See SONG.

Lullaby
A cradle-song, to make a baby sleep.

Madrigal
Italian name for a type of part-song (i.e. polyphonic in style) for a small group of singers, very popular during the Renaissance period, first in Italy, then in England. Most madrigals were secular pieces, but a few were religious.

Magnificat
Religious choral work, basically a setting of the Hymn of the Virgin Mary, sometimes built up into a substantial composition, as by Bach, for chorus, soloists and orchestra.

March
Basically a type of military music for marching to; but slow or funeral marches have formed the basis for some slow movements in symphonies and sonatas.

Masque
Type of stage entertainment with some singing and dancing, related to opera; popular in England during the seventeenth century. The term has occasionally been used since.

Mass
Principal service of the Roman Catholic Church which has been set to music by composers of many different times, and in many different styles. The version usually set to music is known as the 'Ordinary' of the Mass, and consists of five sections—*Kyrie eleison* (Greek 'Lord, have mercy'), *Gloria in excelsis Deo* (Latin 'Glory to God on high'), *Credo* (Latin 'I believe'), *Sanctus* and *Benedictus* (Latin 'Holy' and 'Blessed'), *Agnus Dei* (Latin 'Lamb of God'). The Latin word *Missa* is sometimes used, as in *Missa Solemnis* ('Solemn Mass') and *Missa Brevis* ('Short Mass'). The *Requiem Mass* is a special form of the service, in memory of the dead (*Requiem* means 'repose').

Mazurka
Polish country dance, used by Chopin as the basis for many piano pieces.

Melody
An organized progression of notes of varying pitch, almost always shaped by matters of rhythm and duration; as distinct from HARMONY.

Minuet
Originally a country dance and then a court dance, with three beats to the bar. It was the basis of many movements in eighteenth-century instrumental suites; also formed the basis for the third movement in most symphonies and string quartets of the Classical period.

Minim
Note of duration, equal to two CROTCHETS. The American name is *half-note*.

179

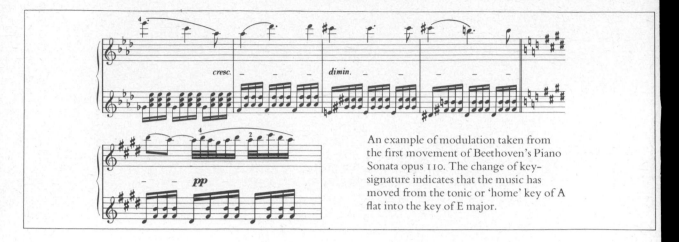

An example of modulation taken from the first movement of Beethoven's Piano Sonata opus 110. The change of key-signature indicates that the music has moved from the tonic or 'home' key of A flat into the key of E major.

Mode
1) Name for each of the SCALES, of Greek origin, which provided the basis for much European music from about the sixth until the sixteenth century;
2) name sometimes given to major and minor scales.

Modulation
To change harmonically from one KEY to another in the course of a single piece of music.

Morris
English folk dance, traditionally played by pipe and drum. The dancers themselves wear bells.

Motet
Type of church choral composition, polyphonic in style, set to religious texts in Latin, and one of the principal forms of composition from about the tenth to the sixteenth century. Since then the name has been given to a much wider variety of compositions, but still nearly always religious in character.

Mute
Device to soften the sound of an instrument, and which almost always modifies its tone as well. In the case of stringed instruments mutes are small clamps placed over the strings at the bridge; with brass instruments they are objects placed in the bell.

Natural
1) In staff NOTATION the sign cancelling previous instructions to sharpen or flatten a note;
2) name sometimes given to a brass wind instrument that has no valves or other mechanical device and so can play only notes belonging to its 'natural' harmonics.

Nocturne
'Night piece', usually a piano piece of a generally quiet, reflective character. This style of nocturne was introduced by the Irish composer John Field, but made famous by Chopin. A few other composers have since used the term.

Nonet
Piece for nine performers, singers or instrumentalists.

Notation
Any system of writing music down, including the TONIC-SOL-FA and TABLATURE, but normally taken to mean the system based on staff lines or STAVES. Here sets of lines across the page (now five in number) provide the framework for the placing of notes on or between the lines, above or below them, as indications of pitch. The exact pitch of the notes is qualified by CLEF, KEY and the use of ACCIDENTALS. Rhythm is indicated by BARS, setting out the measure of the music, and the relative value of notes in terms of duration.

Obbligato
Italian for 'obligatory' or 'compulsory', originally meaning that a part in a piece of music was compulsory; but now sometimes meaning almost the exact opposite, e.g. an instrumental obbligato part to accompany a singer being taken to mean that it is optional.

Octave (8vo)
From the Latin *octo*, 'eight', with reference to the eight notes that make up any major or minor scale. In acoustics any note sounded an exact octave above another has twice the FREQUENCY.

Octet
Piece for eight performers, singers or instrumentalists.

Opera
The word is the plural of the Latin *opus*, 'a work'. It describes the type of musical stage drama that originated in Italy in the early seventeenth century. Basically, most opera consists of dialogue between the singers, interspersed by songs or choruses. In traditional Italian *opera seria* ('serious' or 'tragic opera') and *opera buffa* ('comic opera') the dialogue is declaimed in a special singing style called RECITATIVE; in other kinds of opera, German *singspiel* and French *opéra-comique* (which is not necessarily comic) it is spoken. Wagner dispensed with all

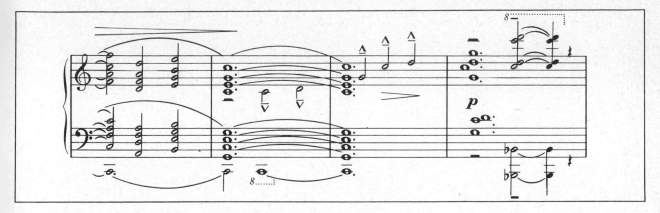

Use of octave signs in Debussy's Piano Prelude *La Cathédrale engloutie*. The notes or chords encompassed by the dotted line are played either an octave lower or higher than written. Note also the tie lines extending the duration of the chords.

such traditions, creating a continuous flow of music, shared between singers and orchestra, which he called 'music-drama'.

Operetta
Italian for 'little opera', describing a much lighter kind of entertainment than true opera, which grew up during the nineteenth century and led to musical comedy and to many stage and film musicals.

Oratorio
Traditionally a kind of religious opera, but without stage action or costumes, owing its name to the fact that the earliest known examples of oratorio were performed in the Oratory of St Philip Neri, Rome, in the early seventeenth century. Today there are some secular choral and vocal works called oratorios, though still of a generally serious and moral character.

Organum
Early form of *polyphony* (i.e. vocal music with two or more melodic lines or 'parts') which grew directly out of PLAINSONG, dating from about the tenth century.

Opus
Latin for 'work', used a great deal in the publication of music, to identify a composition or group of compo-

sitions. The opus numbers given to many seventeenth- and eighteenth-century works may have little connection with their actual order of composition. From the time of Beethoven, they usually do.

Ostinato
Italian for 'obstinate', describing a musical phrase that is repeated over and over again, usually as a form of accompaniment. In jazz BOOGIE uses a very destinctive type of ostinato.

Overture
From the French *ouverture* meaning 'opening', describing a piece of orchestral music played at the opening, i.e. the beginning, of many operas and other stage works. In the nineteenth century the word also began to be applied to short orchestral pieces, usually with some kind of descriptive 'programme' but not connected with any larger stage work. These are known as concert overtures.

Part
An individual melodic line in a piece of music written in a generally polyphonic style. So a four-part FUGUE means a fugue built up on four melodic lines. A *part-song* is one that is made up of individual melodic lines, like a MADRIGAL.

Partita
Italian name for a SUITE in the seventeenth- and eighteenth-century sense of a group of instrumental pieces generally in dance style. Occasionally it can describe a piece in the form of a theme and variations.

Pasadoble
Type of Spanish dance, the word meaning 'double step'.

Passacaglia
An old court dance that developed into a type of composition consisting of variations built upon a constantly repeated theme or motif. In this respect it is similar to a CHACONNE.

Passion
Choral, vocal and orchestral settings of the gospel accounts of Christ's betrayal, trial and crucifixion, similar in form and style to ORATORIO.

Pastoral
Originally the name given to a type of musical stage piece with a rustic theme or setting, but better known today as the special name or nickname given to many compositions which have some connection with the countryside.

Pavan (or Pavane)
Slow, stately court dance of the Renaissance period.

The opening of Debussy's Piano Prelude *Bruyères* ('Heather') with phrase marks indicating how the melody should be shaped, or 'flow'. Note also the various rests.

Phrase

A melodic sequence, usually part of a longer melody. *Phrasing* in a general sense means correctly interpreting the natural flow of the music. *Phrase-marks* in printed music are a guide to this.

Piano (p)

Italian dynamic marking, meaning 'soft'. *Pianissimo* (pp) means 'very soft'.

Pitch

The highness or lowness of a note according to the FREQUENCY (i.e. speed or rapidity) of its vibrations. *Concert-pitch* is the internationally agreed basis for tuning instruments, centred upon the note A above middle C, this being equal to a frequency of 440 cycles per second.

Pizzicato (pizz.)

Italian for 'pinched', but in music an indication for bowed stringed instruments that the strings must be plucked.

Plainsong (or Plainchant)

The style of unaccompanied, unharmonized chanting used in the early Christian church and still to be heard in some Roman Catholic churches and monasteries. The best-known style of plainsong is the Gregorian Chant, named after Pope Gregory I and dating from the sixth century.

Polonaise

French word for 'Polish', describing a fairly stately type of Polish dance, which Chopin transformed into a patriotic-sounding piano piece.

Polyphony

Greek for 'many sounds' or 'many tones', describing methods of composition which involve the interweaving of a number of melodic lines or 'parts'. It was the basis for most Western music for hundreds of years, from about the twelfth to well into the eighteenth century.

Polyrhythm

The playing of music in several rhythms at the same time.

Polytonality

The playing of music in more than one KEY at the same time. Where only two keys are involved it can also be called *bi-tonality*.

Portamento

Italian for 'carrying', describing a style of singing or playing which carries the voice or instrument up or down from one note to the next. Excessive portamento is sometimes called 'scooping'.

Prelude

Strictly this describes a short piece of music that precedes or introduces a more substantial piece, like the prelude to some operas, or the prelude to a fugue. But Chopin and Debussy used the word to describe groups of piano pieces, each piece being self-contained in style and mood.

Presto

Italian tempo marking, meaning 'fast'. *Prestissimo*, 'very fast'.

Programme Music

Descriptive music intended either to evoke a mood or feeling, or to recreate the events of some story. Much nineteenth-century Romantic instrumental and orchestral music has some descriptive 'programme'. The term does not normally apply to opera, ballet or songs, whose music, by its very nature, must be descriptive of something.

Progressive Tonality

The practice of beginning a single piece of music, or a longer work like a symphony, in one KEY and ending in another.

Quartet

Piece for four performers, singers or instrumentalists.

Quaver

Note of duration, half the value of a CROTCHET. The American name is *eighth-note*.

Quintet

Piece for five performers, singers or instrumentalists.

Ragtime
Early jazz style, bright and energetic. Composers and song writers have loosely applied the name to some pieces with a jazz-like character.

Rallentando
Italian tempo marking, meaning 'slow down'.

Recitative
Manner of reciting words in a song-like way, but with more attention to the inflection of the words than to any musical sense of phrasing or rhythm. It usually precedes a proper song, aria or chorus in opera or oratorio. *Recitativo secco* (Italian, 'dry recitative'), as used in much eighteenth-century opera, is delivered quickly with a light instrumental accompaniment, probably a harpsichord. *Recitativo stromentato* ('instrumental recitative') is delivered in a grander style, probably with full orchestral accompaniment.

Reel
A lively kind of dance, traditional to Scotland and Ireland. The Highland Fling is a very energetic kind of Scottish reel.

Requiem
See MASS.

Rest
A period of silence in one or more instrumental or vocal parts, usually equivalent to one or more beats to a bar. Rests are indicated in printed music by signs which correspond to the various notes of duration.

Rhapsody
Name for a piece of music in a fairly free, improvizatory style. It is sometimes given to compositions which are basically a set of variations on a theme.

Rhythm
The beat or pulse of a piece of music, and the distribution of notes within that beat according to their duration.

Semibreve	Minim	Crotchet	Quaver	Semiquaver
𝅝	𝅗𝅥	𝅘𝅥	𝅘𝅥𝅮	𝅘𝅥𝅯
▬	▬	𝄽 or 𝄾	𝄾	𝄿

The principal notes of duration (see page 174) and their corresponding rest signs. Rests can play a vital part in the rhythm of a piece of music.

Ricercare
Italian for 'to seek out', the name for a polyphonic type of instrumental piece usually obeying strict rules of COUNTERPOINT, belonging mainly to the seventeenth century.

Riff
Term used mainly in jazz, swing and dance music to describe a short rhythmic or melodic phrase repeated throughout a piece.

Rigaudon
Old dance from Provence that later became a more courtly French dance. The English equivalent was called a *rigadoon*.

Rock n' Roll
Type of dance music, growing out of the basic 12-bar BLUES form, but with a strong insistent rhythm, which followed SWING in popularity during the 1950s. Bill Haley and his Comets and Elvis Presley were among its greatest stars. The name is taken from the kind of dance movements that went with the music.

Romance
Name given to various pieces of instrumental or orchestral music from the eighteenth century to the present day, indicating more a mood of gentleness and charm than any particular form or style. *Romanza*, the Italian form of the word, is sometimes used.

Rondo
Italian for 'round', describing a piece of music in which one recurring theme (the *rondo theme*) is interspersed with a series of new themes (*episodes*). It is a form that has been used as the last movement of many sonatas, string quartets, symphonies and other instrumental and orchestral works of the Classical period.

Round
From the Latin *rota* 'wheel', describing a simple version of a CANON, almost always for voices, in which each vocal 'part' joins in turn, singing the same melody in the same key, all following each other round until each decides to end.

Rubato
Italian for 'robbed', describing a way of playing a piece of music with a certain degree of licence with regard to tempo and phrasing; in other words the player 'robs' some notes of a little of their true duration in order to give a little extra to others. Some rubato is necessary in the performance of most kinds of music, if it is not to sound stiff and wooden.

Rumba
Latin American, especially Cuban, dance that was very popular as a ballroom dance in the 1930s and 1940s. The rhythm of the rumba has occasionally been used by composers, notably Gershwin.

Saltarello
Italian folk dance, lively and energetic, used as the basis for the last movement of Mendelssohn's *Italian* Symphony.

Samba
Latin American dance, similar to a RUMBA.

Sarabande
Old courtly dance, originating in Spain, often included in seventeenth- and eighteenth-century instrumental suites.

Scale
From the Italian *scala* 'stairway' or 'step', describing various sequences of notes which progress step by step in PITCH and provide the basis for systems of music, i.e. music is composed from a selection of the available notes in one or other scale or groups of scales. We are most familiar with the major and minor scales, divided up into OCTAVE sections, each conforming to the same sequence of pitch intervals; but other systems of scale have been the old church MODES, each with its own special sequence of pitch intervals; the *pentatonic* scale of only five notes (corresponding in terms of pitch intervals to the black notes on a piano keyboard) which has formed the basis of much folk music in different parts of the world; and the CHROMATIC scale forming the basis of TWELVE-TONE composition.

Scat Singing
A jazz style of singing in which the voice does not sing words but imitates the rhythm and tone of other instruments. The old Celtic, especially Scottish, 'mouth music' was similar in its intentions.

Scherzo
Italian for 'joke'.
1) Describing a much speeded up and more dynamic version of the MINUET which Beethoven introduced as the third movement to most of his symphonies, and in some of his instru-mental works;
2) the name for other fairly fast and dramatic instrumental or orchestral pieces, not necessarily in the same rhythm as the Beethoven-style scherzo.

Semibreve
Note of duration and the longest in normal use today, twice the value of the MINIM, four times that of the CROTCHET. The American name is *whole-note*.

Semiquaver
Note of duration, half the value of a QUAVER, or one quarter the value of a CROTCHET. The American name is *sixteenth-note*.

Semitone
'Half tone', the smallest interval of PITCH normally used in Western music. With reference to a piano keyboard, examples of semitones are from any note E to the adjacent F, F to F sharp, B to C.

Septet
Piece for seven performers, instrumentalists or singers.

Sequence
1) The repetition of a musical phrase at a different PITCH, probably meaning in a different KEY;
2) type of hymn in the Roman Catholic Church, its origins going back to the early days of polyphony and departure from PLAINSONG.

Serenade
'Night piece', the opposite of an AUBADE, but a name applied to many different pieces of music, usually intended as light entertainment. In the Classical period of the eighteenth century it often described an instru-mental or orchestral piece of several movements, almost like a small symphony, as in Mozart's *Eine Kleine Nachtmusik* ('A Little Night Music').

Serial Music
Music based on any selected series of notes, but applying mainly to TWELVE-TONE composition.

Sextet
Piece for six players, instrumentalists or singers.

Sforzando (sf)
Italian 'reinforced', a dynamic marking, meaning that a note or chord should be played with special emphasis.

Sharp
Sign indicating that a note must be raised in pitch by a SEMITONE.

Sinfonia
Early name for a symphony, sometimes given to overtures. In the eighteenth century a *sinfonia concertante* was a sort of cross between a symphony and concerto, an orchestral work in several movements with solo parts for a small group of instruments. *Sinfonietta*, 'little sinfonia', describing a small, light-weight symphony, sometimes used also as the name for a small orchestra.

Solmization
Any method of keeping a written record of music by the use of syllables as distinct from *staff notation*. The best-known method is the *Tonic Sol-Fa* in which the syllables doh, ray, me, fah, soh, lah, te, doh represent the order of notes in a scale and not their actual pitch. Doh (the first, or TONIC note in a scale) can stand for any chosen note, and the other notes in a simple tune, as expressed by their syllable, follow from it. Such methods, which are really memory aids, date back to the eleventh century and the ideas of Guido d'Arezzo.

Solo
Performance by one person.

Sonata
From the Italian *suonare* 'to sound', an instrumental piece originating in the seventeenth century; reaching its

best-known form in the Classical period of the eighteenth century as a composition for a solo keyboard instrument, or keyboard and one other solo instrument, usually in three movements. During the nineteenth century this form was further modified or expanded by Beethoven, Liszt and others.

Sonata Form
Special way of organizing a single piece of music which evolved during the Classical period of the eighteenth century. It is basically in three sections—Exposition (presentation of themes and other musical ideas), Development (literally meaning the development or modification of those existing themes and ideas), Recapitulation (a return to the music of the Exposition but usually with some modification as to key). Sonata form provides the basis for many first movements of instrumental sonatas, trios and string quartets, orchestral concertos and symphonies. It is sometimes applied to other movements.

Song
Vocal composition as distinct from choral, often for one voice only, but sometimes for a small group of singers, in which case it may be a part-song with a separate melodic line or part for each singer. Songs exist under many different names, e.g. CANZONA, CHANSON, AYRE, MADRIGAL. The German word *Lied* is usually applied to the great tradition of song writing among German-speaking composers of the Romantic period—Schubert, Schumann, Mendelssohn, Brahms, Wolf.

Soprano
1) Highest range in pitch of a woman's voice. *Mezzo-soprano* 'half soprano', not so high in pitch as a true soprano;
2) the name of a clef.

Sostenuto
Italian 'sustained', an instruction for music to be played smoothly.

Spiritual
Name for religious folk songs of the American Negroes as they used to live and work on the cotton plantations. Like their work songs, spirituals often took the form of solo passages followed by a chorus.

Stabat Mater
Originally a type of hymn dealing with the Virgin Mary and the Crucifixion, and the basis for larger choral compositions by several composers.

Staccato
Italian 'detached', describing the method of playing notes in a quick, detached way, indicated on printed music by a dot over the notes.

Stave (or Staff)
Name for each of the lines drawn horizontally in sets of five across music paper and forming the basis of *staff notation*. See also NOTATION.

Stomp
Early jazz style, lively and energetic.

Strophic
Name for a type of song that repeats the same music (perhaps with a little modification) for each verse or stanza of the poem which it is based upon.

Suite
From the French *suivre* 'to follow', describing:
1) an instrumental composition of the seventeenth and eighteenth centuries which was a succession of pieces based on dance forms;
2) an orchestral composition of the nineteenth and twentieth centuries which is either a shortened form of a larger score (often of a ballet), or a group of pieces usually linked by some particular idea or image.

Swing
Dance music of the 1930s and 1940s, developed from jazz and characterized by strong, syncopated rhythms.

Symphonic Poem
Type of orchestral composition, created by Liszt, which has some descriptive programme, and little to do with normal symphonic form.

Symphony
Name taken from the Greek meaning 'sounding together'. It was applied in Renaissance and Baroque times to many pieces of music for a group of instrumentalists; but during the Classical period of the eighteenth century it developed out of existing forms of operatic overture to become the most important kind of orchestral composition, usually of four movements—fairly fast (perhaps with a slow introduction), slow, minuet with a central section called a trio, and fast. Haydn perfected this form, Beethoven greatly enlarged it, and in terms of size and complexity the symphony reached its most expanded form in the works of Mahler. Originally for orchestra alone, symphonies from Beethoven onward have sometimes included a choir and vocal soloists also.

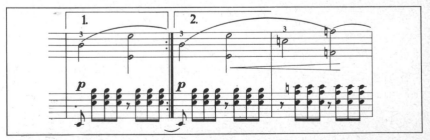

In Sonata Form, first- and second-time bars indicate when the music of the Exposition should be repeated before proceeding into the Development section (first movement of Beethoven's Piano Sonata opus 14 no 1).

Syncopation. This violin passage from the first movement of Beethoven's *Eroica* Symphony clearly shows the emphasis of the beat shifting from one bar to the next. The basic rhythm of the music is three crotchet beats to the bar.

Syncopation

Term used in rhythm to describe the shifting of emphasis from the established beat of a piece of music, including the placing of emphasis between the beats of the bar. Used by many composers, but developing its most distinctive form in JAZZ and SWING.

Tablature

Type of NOTATION, usually applied to stringed instruments, that instructs the player by symbols or diagrams where to place his fingers in order to obtain the required notes or chords. Tablature was used in Renaissance times for lutenists, and is mainly used today for the guitar.

Tango

Latin American dance rhythm, originating in Argentina, which became tremendously popular as a form of ballroom dancing in Europe and the United States during the 1920s.

Tarantella

Fast and lively dance from southern Italy, associated both with the town of Taranto and the tarantula spider. The dance was supposed either to be caused by the creature's bite or to be a cure for it.

Te Deum

More fully in Latin *Te Deum laudamus* ('We praise thee, O God'), the basis for important choral works.

Temperament

Word to describe methods of tuning, especially in connection with keyboard instruments and their ability to play in all the major and minor keys.

Tempo

Italian for 'time', but the word is more often concerned with the pace or speed of a piece of music rather than time in terms of rhythmic beats to the bar.

Tenor

Word derived from the Latin *tenere* 'to hold', because in some polyphonic music the main melodic line was taken or 'held' by a high-voiced male singer. It now describes:
1) the highest-pitched range of men's voices;
2) the range of pitch of a particular instrument among a family of instruments, e.g. tenor saxophone;
3) the name of a clef.

Timbre

see TONE.

Time-signature

In NOTATION, the indication of the basic rhythm of a bar or bars within a piece of music. It looks like an arithmetical fraction. The top figure gives the number of beats to the bar, the bottom figure indicates how the beats should be measured, e.g. as CROTCHETS, QUAVERS, MINIMS or other notes of duration.

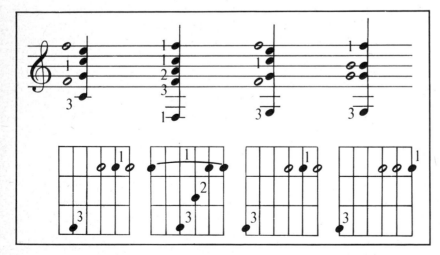

Tablature for the guitar showing finger positions on the fret-board to obtain each chord. Numbers indicate which finger to use on each string. Circles indicate an 'open' (i.e. unstopped) string.

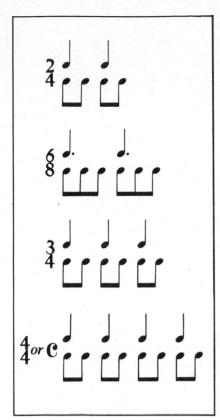

Three familiar time-signatures: two crotchets to the bar: six quavers to the bar; four crotchets to the bar (or Common Time, sometimes simply marked C).

Toccata
From the Italian *toccare* 'to touch', describing a piece of keyboard music basically designed to test the player's finger control and touch.

Tone
1) The quality of a musical sound, also called by the French word *timbre*; 2) the pitch interval between two adjacent notes as placed on a piano keyboard, i.e. whole-tone or SEMITONE; 3) the usual American name for a note.

Tonic
The first, or leading note in any of the major or minor scales, giving its name to the scale in question. The word is also sometimes used to refer to the KEY in which a piece of music is written, especially when the music has modulated out of the tonic, or home key and then returns to it. The *tonic sol-fa* is a system for learning a melody by memorizing the relationship between the notes rather than their individual pitch. See SOLMIZATION.

Transcription
To make a new instrumental or vocal arrangement of a piece of music. There are many famous transcriptions, including J.S. Bach's arrangement of Vivaldi's Concerto for Four Violins for four harpsichords, Leopold Stokowski's orchestral transcription of Bach's Organ Toccata and Fugue in D minor, and Ravel's orchestral version of Mussorgsky's piano composition *Pictures at an Exhibition*. Composers sometimes transcribe their own works.

Transposition
To change the pitch in which a piece of music is played or sung. In practice this usually means performing the music in a different KEY from the original. *Transposing Instruments* are those which produce notes at a fixed interval of pitch below or above the notes as they are written in a score. In the case of a so-called B-flat clarinet, for example, the instrument sounds the note B flat when the player is reading note C in the score, and it constantly produces notes one tone lower than those written. Such a situation exists because clarinets, and many other woodwind and brass instruments, were traditionally tuned to one particular key.

Treble
1) The highest range of pitch of a boy's voice; 2) the range of pitch of a particular instrument among a family of instruments, e.g. treble recorder; 3) the name of a clef.

Trill
The best-known type of musical ornamentation, created by the rapid alternative playing or singing of two notes, a whole TONE or SEMITONE apart. Indicated in music by the abbreviation 'tr' and a wavy line.

Trio
Piece for three performers, instrumentalists or singers.

Trope
Name for variations made to the melody or words in medieval plainsong and very early polyphonic singing.

Tutti
Italian for 'all', a term used to describe a passage for full orchestra, or full chorus, after one involving only soloists or a small group of players or singers. In a concerto it may simply mean a passage for the orchestra, whether or not everyone is actually playing, in contrast to a passage for the soloist.

Twelve-Tone Music
Music based not on one of the established major or minor keys, but on a particular sequence using all twelve notes of the CHROMATIC SCALE as they exist within an OCTAVE. Schoenberg was the first to develop this type of SERIAL composition, also called DODECAPHONIC music, and it has had a great influence on the music of this century.

Vamp
Very basic sort of instrumental accompaniment to a song, often by a pianist playing by ear.

Variation Form
More fully a theme and variations, consisting firstly of the theme or melody in question, and then of various musical treatments of it. In the seventeenth and eighteenth centuries, sets of variations often involved little more than different

musical decorations of the theme, but Beethoven and composers after him used variation form as an expression of their finest creative ingenuity. It has frequently been used as the slow movement of symphonies, concertos, string quartets and sonatas, sometimes also as the basis for the last movements of such works.

Vibrato

Italian 'vibrated', describing a slight variation in pitch of the sounding of a note, mainly involving singers and players of bowed stringed instruments. A little vibrato is attractive to modern ears (there were times in the past when it was not encouraged), but too much becomes a wobble.

Virtuoso

A performer, usually referring to an instrumentalist, of exceptional technical skill. The term can apply also to music specially associated with demonstrations of such skill.

Vivace

Italian term of mood or expression, meaning 'lively'.

Voluntary

Usually an organ piece played at the beginning or end of church services, sometimes played from music, sometimes improvized.

Waltz

Dance form with three steady but lilting beats to the bar, possibly the most popular of all dances; occasionally used as a movement in a symphony, e.g. by Berlioz and Tchaikovsky.

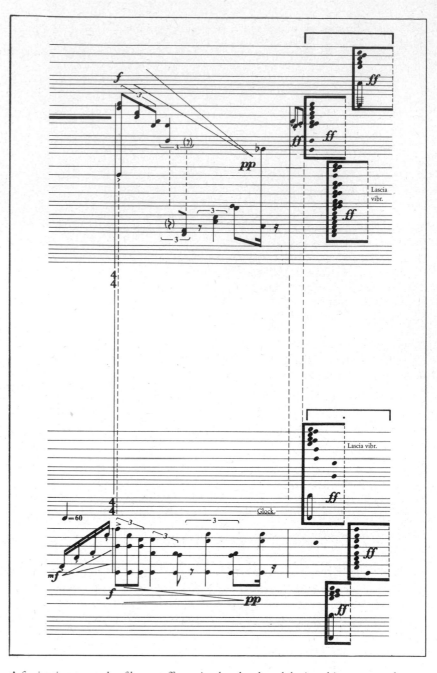

A fascinating example of how staff notation has developed during this century, taken from the score of *Circles* by the Italian composer Luciano Berio (born 1925). The work is for soprano, harp and percussion, and requires the soloist to clap her hands and move about the concert platform as well as sing.

Acknowledgements

The author wishes to acknowledge the information and useful reference material which he found in the following works:

Big Band Jazz, Albert McCarty (Barrie and Jenkins); *The Bodley Head History of Western Music*, Christopher Headington; *A Concise History of Music*, Percy M. Young (Benn); *Concise Oxford Dictionary of Music*, Percy A. Scholes; *Kobbes Complete Opera Book*, Ed. The Earl of Harewood (Putnam); *Lives of the Great Composers*, Harold Schonberg (Davis-Poynter); *Man and His Music*, Alec Harman and Wilfred Mellers (Barrie and Jenkins); *Music at Court*, Christopher Hogwood (Folio Society); *Music Since the First World War*, Arnold Whittall (Dent); *New Penguin Dictionary of Music*, Arthur Jacob; *Old Musical Instruments*, Rene Clemeuric (Weidenfied and Nicolson); *A Plain Man's Guide to Jazz*, John Postgate (Honour Books Ltd.).

All colour illustrations, apart from that on page 73, are reproduced by kind permission of Fabbri Editori.
Illustrations are also credited to the following sources:

Academy Gallery, Venice, ii; Albi Museum Paris, 81; R. Ambor, 87*l*; Anger Museum, 33*l*; Associated Recording Company, 83; Erich Auerbach, 133*t*, 140*r*, 143*r*, 144, 148, 149*l*, 159, 161*r*; BBC, 121; Beethovenhaus, Bonn, 47; Bertarelli Collection Milan, 59*r*; Bibliotecca dell'Escorial, Madrid, 16*l*, 16*r*, 17*l*, 17*r*; Bibliothèque Nationale, Paris, 62, 89, 96*b*; British Museum, London, 9; Carnavalet Museum, Paris, 44; Keith Cheerman/Schott, 165; Doria Turst Palace, Genoa, 54*r*; Downtown Gallery, New York, 84; Egyptian Museum, Torino, 8; Electronic Music Studios (London) Ltd, 123; EMI Records Ltd, 139*l*; Photo EPS, 10; Estense Library, Modena, 19; Farinelli Private Collection, Rome, 88; Courtesy of the Finnish Consulate, 66*tr*; M.L. Gioia, 90; Burt Goldblatt, 83; Houston Rogers, 192, 160*l*; Jazz Music Books, London, 126, 169; Knitze Collection, New York, 78*r*; La Scala Theatrical Museum, Milan, 61*l*, 61*r*, 63, 65, 66*bl*, 68, 72, 76, 92*tl*, 92*tr*, 92*b*, 96*t*; O. Langini, 79*l*; *Life* Magazine, 82; London Features International, 122, 178*r*; Louvre Museum, Paris 52*r*, 74; Colin Maher, 100; Mansell Collection, London, 130*r*; Mendelssohn Archive, Berlin, 54*l*; André Meyer Collection, Paris, 53; Monaco Opera House, 95; Monza Cathedral 15*l*; Mozart Museum, Salzburg, 46; Municipal Museum, Bologna, 41, 42; Museum of Central Africa, Brussels, 12; Museum of Decorative Art, Paris, 70; Museum of Musical Instruments, Brussels, 31; Museum of Musical Instruments, Milan, 27, 34, 36*t*; 40*b*; Museum of Naples 29; Museum di Risorgimento, Udine, 49; Opera Theatre, Rome, 94; National Gallery, London, 23, 32, National Gallery, Oslo, 67; National Gallery, Paris, 32, 69*r*; National Library, Vienna, 15*r*, 45, 55; National Museum, Warsaw, 77; National Portrait Gallery, London, 134*r*, 136*r*, 152*r*, 154*r*, 167, 170; Penguin Books Ltd, Walker & Co., New York, 102*r*; R. Polillo 87*r*; Popperfoto 125*l*, 125*r*, 134*l*, 139*r*, 153, 161*l*, 171; Private Collection 40*t*; Rezzonico Museum, Venice, 39; Ricordi Archive, Milan, 64; Royal College of Music, London, 130*l*; 131, 132, 133*b*, 136*l*, 137*l*, 137*r*, 138, 140*l*, 143*l*, 145, 146, 151*l*, 151*r*, 152*l*, 155*t*, 155*b*, 156, 157, 158*t*, 158*b*, 160*r*, 162*l*, 162*r*, 163*l*, 163*r*, 164, 166; Royal Opera House, London, 147, 154*l*; Jack Russo, Milan, 87*b*; San Pietro Conservatory, Naples, 29; Schack Gallery, Monaco, 52*l*; G. Schirmer Ltd, 127; Schubert Museum, Vienna, 51; S.E.F. Torino 7; Smetana Museum, Prague, 66*tl*; Society of Musicians, Vienna, 56, 60, Steinway & Co. 117; Charlie Stewart 85, 86, Théâtre de la Monnaie, Brussels, 75; Theatre Museum, London/Crown copyright, 104*b*, 135, 149*r*, 150, 168; Tretiakov Gallery, Moscow, 69*l*; Trivulziana Library, Milan, 20; Turku Music Museum, Finland, iii; Uffizi Gallery, Firenze, 22; USIS, Paris, 80; Verdi Conservatory, Milan, 93; Verdi Museum, Milan, 62; Victoria and Albert Museum, London, 71, 73, 98, 99*l*; 101, 102*l*, 103*r*, 103*l*, 104*t*, 105*l*, 105*r*, 106*l*, 106*r*, 107, 108, 109*l*, 109*r*, 110*l*, 110*r*, 111, 112, 113*l*, 113*r*, 115*t*, 115*b*, 116; Vienna Museum, 50, 78*l*; Wagner Commemoration Centre, Bayreuth, 57*l*, 57*r*, 58; Wagner Museum, Lucerne, 59*l*; Ward Lock Ltd, London, 98, 118, 141; Zurich Municipal Theatre, 79*r*.

Index